MARKETING
FROM THE INSIDE OUT ®

Transformational growth for
purpose-driven leaders

WENDY MAYNARD & SHAWN BUSSE

kinesis

Published by Kinesis
1627 NW 14th Ave.
Portland, OR 97209

© 2018 Kinesis

ISBN: 978-0-692-94922-1 (paperback)
ISBN: 978-0-692-95042-5 (ebook)

CONTENTS

PREFACE

IN RETROSPECT, THERE WERE PROBABLY BETTER TIMES TO OPEN a small business than January 2000.

While our fledgling marketing company wasn't directly affected by the dot-com collapse, the countless stories we were hearing about so many of the hottest young companies failing weren't exactly confidence-inspiring.

But we do have the bubble to thank for one important thing: it helped us understand that no company could ever be truly immune from changes in the economic landscape. We might not have been directly affected by the bubble, but that didn't mean we wouldn't be affected by some other economic shake-up.

(More about that in a bit . . .)

This realization drove us to make our first strategic decision about Kinesis. Our goal had always been to help companies grow through their branding, marketing, and design efforts—but watching the news helped us recognize that we'd also need to take larger economic trends into account if we wanted to really thrive in good times and bad.

And so, we decided to focus on professional services businesses— in particular, medical practices. It was a growing industry that was largely buffered from outside economic assaults, and one that had a large presence in our area. (In southern Oregon, where our first office was located, there was an aging retirement population and a vibrant health care community of expert physicians who'd moved there for the quality of life.)

We also learned to choose client companies that were built with a clear business structure in place. It seemed to us that what so many of the dot-coms lacked was that discipline—and so we focused on organizations with clear business methodologies run by people who were professional experts in their fields.

While this was a good foundation, it wasn't enough to grow our business in a long-term, sustainable fashion. And it certainly didn't create a competitive advantage for Kinesis. But we didn't realize that at the time.

> "Sometimes when you innovate, you make mistakes. It is best to admit them quickly, and get on with improving your other innovations."
>
> —Steve Jobs

We'll be very honest with you. Along with some good decisions, we also made a lot of cringe-worthy choices in our early days. Most small business owners do—and many of us don't bounce back from those mistakes. According to the U.S. Bureau of Labor Statistics and the U.S. Small Business Administration, only half of all new establishments survive five years or more, and about one-third last ten years or more—this figure has not changed significantly over time.[1]

We hope that the ideas we share with you here will help you be one of the success stories and save you some of the pain we experienced as we launched and began to grow.

When Kinesis first opened its doors, we operated in a similar fashion to many professional-service companies. Like most creative firms, we produced brochures, marketing plans, advertisements, logos, and websites. After each project was completed, we would often have the opportunity to engage in a new project with our clients if they had another request.

Perhaps the scenario sounds familiar to you. If you are part of a professional services firm or another type of business-to-business (B2B) company with long sales cycles and high levels of service, then there's a good chance you have a very similar business model.

There are a number of pitfalls in this type of approach, which we explore later in the book.

For now, suffice to say in the beginning of our business we were basically order-takers for our clients because we weren't leading the conversations with innovative solutions. And, because we hadn't differentiated ourselves in any meaningful way, our marketing and design services were little better than a commodity. At the time, Kinesis also had no process for keeping clients retained—we were stuck in an endless cycle of sales—proposals—projects with all of the up-and-down cash flow issues that come with this approach.

Still, we were slowly growing—and that was exciting. We were also watching the marketing landscape become radically more complex. Thanks to the Web 2.0 phenomenon[2] which gave internet users countless opportunities to engage, the old models of schmoozing on the golf course, placing ads in newspapers, and waiting for the phone to ring were becoming increasingly irrelevant (hello, Yellow Pages?).

The business leaders we were meeting with told us time and again how traditional models were failing them. Whether they had an in-house marketing person, outsourced freelancers, or hired a tactical agency, their marketing plans were gathering dust because they couldn't keep up with the internet's rapidly shifting technology.

In addition, there were no real models for them to turn to. Since most marketing books are filled with Fortune 500 case studies, the strategies our clients were reading about just weren't helping them overcome the hurdles they actually faced.

We came to the conclusion that marketing models for the small- to mid-size businesses that we served were broken.

Which meant we did something about it immediately. Right?

Well, not exactly.

Despite our realization, we kept doing what we were doing because—in all honesty—it was pretty easy to continue serving up orders of "a website, logo, with a very small side order of consulting." We were relatively plump and happy as a business, and we didn't have to stretch ourselves much to get more of the same.

And then 2008 happened.

We fooled ourselves into thinking Kinesis hadn't really experienced any impact from the Great Recession. After all, by the end of October 2009, we had about twenty-five contracts out to tried-and-true client companies, as well as some new companies that looked like they would need marketing projects in 2010.

But then November came and went. And December. None of our pending contracts were signed. This had never happened before, but our clients and prospects assured us that "management was waiting until the beginning of Q1 to approve new work" and "as soon as XYZ customer pays us, we'll get this contract signed."

Before we knew it, it was January and, still, nothing was signed. One client who owed us a lot of money from work in 2008 declared bankruptcy without paying us the thousands of dollars we were counting on. As a result of the lack of this payment and no new work, we had to dip deeply into our line of credit to float payroll.

This will come as no surprise to those of you whose companies were battered by the economic crisis, but it got uglier from there. We fell into even deeper debt and were forced to lay off our beloved long-term employees. Kinesis delayed payments to our vendors begging their forgiveness. And we stopped taking salaries.

We tell you all of these things not because we want sympathy, but because we want you to understand where we've been before we explain where Kinesis is at today. We want you to know where our inspirations and formulas came from because without this despair, we never would have made the leap we did. We never would have set our Big Vision:

"To be the company that changes the way
businesses use marketing to do
good in the world."

OUR "HAIL MARY" PASS

AS WE TOOK A GOOD LOOK AT OUR Q1 FINANCIALS FOR 2010, our debt load, and our anorexic projections for the rest of the year, we had to be honest with ourselves. Our company was in a downward spiral with no clear sign of recovery. And so, we decided it was time for a "Hail Mary" pass:

We decided to act on our true convictions that marketing for small- to mid-size businesses is fundamentally broken.

We recognized that even though the marketing landscape has changed radically, the systems for managing marketing haven't kept up. Moreover, for SMBs, there are few resources to help you scale. While we love Jim Collins, Tom Peters, Peter Drucker, and W. Chan Kim, their books are often filled with case studies aimed at much larger businesses. Their ideas simply weren't working for our clients. They didn't scale down correctly.

And so, we decided to test our theory that marketing needed to link arms with both human resources and leadership. It was time to tie-in the brand to margins, bottom-line revenue, leadership, and culture.

Drawing from the ideas of many great business leaders and our own experiences from more than a decade of working with SMBs, we developed a system called Marketing From the Inside Out® that is both a philosophy and a business development model.

It's an approach that weaves marketing and sales to employee engagement, leadership, performance, and great service so these functions no longer exist in silos. Marketing From the Inside Out® shows companies how to carve out a true competitive advantage that attracts leads *and* talent.

It may sound unbelievable to you and you probably want to know, "Did our new model work?"

We're thrilled to say it did—amazingly well. Our client companies thrived. They grew more profitable and their revenues climbed. Their cultures improved, as did both employee retention and customer loyalty. From the leadership to the front-line staff, people enjoyed work more. And because they were cherry-picking their dream customers, they enjoyed the people they served as well.

For example, in just two years, one of our clients increased client acquisition by more than 40 percent and reduced client churn *and* employee turnover to almost zero. Another client realized a 127 percent revenue growth over two years. Still another increased its average contract size by more than 50 percent.

This was a direct result of carving out a clear competitive advantage and increasing the focus on hiring the *right* people who were engaged and motivated to grow the company. Their leadership team's commitment to the mission and values of the organization resulted in amazing customer service, which lead to an increased customer spend and greatly improved customer retention, leading to a higher average customer lifetime value.

And we, too, began to succeed at a level we never thought possible. As a result of our clients' successes, Kinesis not only hired back the employees we had been forced to lay off during our most difficult period, but we've added multiple new team members and are continuing to grow.

As we implemented the same philosophies we share with our clients, we've watched our own culture thrive. Kinesis was able to move to a beautiful new space. Our company has been on the list of Oregon's Fastest Growing 100 Companies five consecutive times, has become a Certified B Corporation, and in 2014 was presented with the Small Business Innovation Award from the *Portland Business Journal*.

Our Big Vision is to help change the world through the power of small business marketing. We believe that business owners—connected to their community, their customers, and their employees— are the best hope for lasting change in our society. So, we decided to write this book to share our Marketing From the Inside Out® methodology as widely as possible.

Let's dive in.

MARKETING FROM THE INSIDE OUT® PRINCIPLES

INTRODUCTION

ON A CLOUDY FRIDAY AFTERNOON IN LATE SEPTEMBER, Charles Gratton looks around at his half-empty office. A few consultants sit staring at their computers—heads down, headphones on. With no sounds other than the ambient noise of computers and air conditioning, Charles's office has the feel of a library.

A tall man with messy dark hair, glasses, and a plaid shirt, Charles turns and walks back into his corner office. He shuts the door quietly behind him and takes a seat. As he gazes out his window at the city below, he asks himself, "How did I get here *again*?"

He spent the past week letting half of his staff go. Unsurprisingly, those that remain feel stressed, dejected, and generally unhappy. As a rule, his employees rarely communicate with one another and typically work plugged into their headphones while working on their computers. While the consultants are hard workers, there is little camaraderie among the employees. Overall, Charles doesn't think the people who work for him seem very satisfied.

And, when he allows himself to slow down enough to think about it, Charles has to admit that he's pretty unhappy too.

Typically, he's an affable fellow who loves to talk about his big ideas. His sharp mind and ability to connect with new prospects help him land large projects pretty easily. Unfortunately, Charles also has a tendency to oversell his team's capacity to deliver. More often than not, he finds himself scrambling to hire consulting contractors who can come in with rapid-fire expertise in order to finish a job. But because these contractors are expensive and rarely want to become employees after the project is over, this tactic has not been particularly profitable. Plus, his full-time employees' enthusiasm for projects and clients seems lukewarm when multiple contractors come in to share the work.

As a result of his approach, Charles's company, Apex, has gone through several boom-then-bust cycles. After a big project, when there is a gap in new work and cash flow, Charles not only has to let his contractors go but is sometimes forced to fire multiple employees who he can no longer support.

That's where he is this September afternoon—stuck in a down cycle, working to land the next big project. His team lacks morale and he knows it will be hard to hire the right people when the next big project comes in.

Charles doesn't understand why he is in this situation again—he just wants to create work for his people and bring home money to support his family. That's why he always takes on whatever projects come his way.

Until this point, Charles has operated under the premise that he has a simple marketing problem. He has believed that if he could just get the word out to more businesses and generate more leads then Apex would have all the cash they need to keep growing and hiring. In the past, he has tried hiring search engine optimization

(SEO) agencies and lead generation firms and salespeople. He even had a new website designed last year.

But inevitably, he has ended up in the same position. So, should he—once again—throw a lot of money into customer acquisition?

Charles wonders if there is a better approach.

Could Apex attract a steadier stream of clients? Could they start taking on a greater number of smaller projects that last longer—as opposed to hunting for clients only when revenues dip? Could he avoid the cycle of 70 percent revenue growth followed by 65 percent dips?

And is there a way to build a stronger culture? Can we create a work environment that feels less like a library? Can we make a place that he and his colleagues look forward to coming to every day? Can he attract more committed employees—people who care about the future of the company, not just their paycheck?

At the heart of all these questions was one big one:

How could Apex develop a better brand reputation—both as a service provider and as an employer—so instead of spending all his time and energy chasing down a big "elephant" every time revenues dip, potential clients seek out Apex instead?

Too many companies look a lot like Apex: They do a little of this and a little of that. They'll never say no to a project. They swing back and forth between rapid growth and extreme streamlining. Their culture is mediocre and the organization struggles with poor employee performance and high turnover. The focus is more on top-line revenue than profits. The owners don't know where their next customers are coming from, causing sleepless nights worrying about cash flow.

But there is a better way.

BEYOND BUSINESS AS USUAL:
AN INTEGRATED BUSINESS ECOSYSTEM

THE APPROACH THAT APEX CEO CHARLES GRATTON HAS taken with his company isn't unusual. Far from it—it's quite common.

Many company owners and leaders believe the way to run a business is to focus solely on growing revenue for shareholders instead of viewing the entire business as a complex, interrelated ecosystem. Now, in smaller companies, there may not be any "shareholders" beyond the owners—but that doesn't mean this isn't still a problem that impacts everyone at the organization.

This approach to running a company is born out of a concept known as "shareholder primacy" or the "shareholder value theory"—an idea whose popularity many trace back to economist Milton Friedman's influential 1970 *New York Times* op-ed piece[3] and furthered by academics Michael C. Jensen and William H. Meckling in 1976.[4]

Friedman wrote, "There is one and only one social responsibility of business—to use its resources and engage in activities designed to increase its profits so long as it . . . engages in open and free competition, without deception or fraud."[5]

The idea at the core of the theory is that companies succeed when their leaders grow top-line revenue through marketing, sales, and employee growth. To "win" at the business game and bring more money to shareholders, leaders drive their companies to grow, no matter the cost to the culture and its people.

There is ample evidence that shareholder primacy results in chronic short-termism, income inequality, a disengaged and poorly trained workforce who are treated as disposable, shortchanged customers, and endemic malfeasance. And yet, this notion continues to be predominant—even though history has shown us again and again that the "shareholder value theory" fails even on its single rule of *make more money.*[6] And, at its very worst, it results in corruption such as the notorious scandals in 2001 and 2002 with Enron, WorldCom, Tyco International, Global Crossing, and Adelphia, the options back-dating scandals of 2005 and 2006, and the subprime meltdown of 2007 and 2008.[7]

Even Jack Welch, former CEO of General Electric (GE), who is regarded as the father of the "shareholder value game"—and, by all accounts, "won" this game at GE—now disparages the approach. In 2009, he gave an interview with Francesco Guerrera of the *Financial Times* and said: "On the face of it, shareholder value is the dumbest idea in the world. Shareholder value is a result, not a strategy . . . your main constituencies are your employees, your customers, and your products."[8]

Despite widespread criticism, the obsession with maximizing shareholder value has taken on a cult-like following in many large public companies. Without having other prominent models to follow, small- to mid-sized businesses emulate their larger brethren.

But this is a flawed way of leading a company. And it's an approach that creates a company like Apex—one with disengaged employees, unhappy owners, and dissatisfied customers. And—paradoxically—less revenue and profits over the long term.

The Apex story highlights a hidden problem—an issue that is critical for small business success but often neglected: when leadership fails to see that their commitment should be to *all* of its stakeholders (rather than merely its owners or shareholders) they're effectively building a "house" with no internal structure.

Because CEOs like Charles Gratton focus only on growing revenues and not on creating a thriving ecosystem driven to serve its customers, employees, and surrounding communities, their companies will suffer from multiple boom-and-bust cycles and they will have trouble with both client and talent retention. Plus, they may feel like Charles and not even own a place *they* enjoy working.

Fortunately, some leaders of large companies are starting to speak out against the shareholder primacy theory.

"As practiced today, capitalism too often becomes a race to the bottom. In low-growth economies, a focus on earnings-per-share (EPS) is leading to more unemployment and deepening inequality," wrote Marc Benioff, CEO of Salesforce, in a *Huffington Post* article. "The renowned economist Milton Friedman preached that the business of business is to engage in activities designed to increase profits. He was wrong. The business of business isn't just about creating profits for shareholders—it's also about improving the state of the world and driving stakeholder value."

We think this wisdom is equally vital for small- to medium-sized businesses. An approach that puts focus on all shareholders takes more time and dedication up front, but it results in sustained business growth, more profits, and better retention of both employees and customers. Building a business in this manner is all about running a marathon, not a sprint.

In fact, we think this long-term approach to building, growing, and marketing a company is the only one that makes sense:

> Sustained business success is determined by creating a company that has an integrated ecosystem of engaged customers, engaged leadership, and engaged customers with a core mission, values, vision, and strategy to guide them.

> We call this approach "Marketing From the Inside Out®."

Marketing From the Inside Out® is a methodology that helps companies transform their organization into one that is purpose driven, person focused, and community oriented. They strive to be the best for all of their stakeholders.

As leaders, we each have a choice. We can build a company that grows at any cost, burning ourselves and our people out along the way.

Or, we can grow our organization from the inside out.

Companies that grow from the inside out:

1. Have a solid mission that guides every decision that every person in their company makes.
2. Have well-defined core values that their people live and breathe every single day.
3. Have a Big Vision that directs where they are going.
4. Prioritize systems that weave their mission, values, and vision through the entire fabric of their company.

Leadership teams at these companies focus a great deal of energy on building a great culture with the right-fit people. They take the time to develop processes and systems to support both employees and customers. They focus on making a company a great place for *all* of their stakeholders (and they reject shareholder primacy).

If you are sitting there scratching your head thinking "I thought I picked up a book about marketing; what's all this about culture and people?" stick with us. In our experience, any marketing that does not take into account internal customers and everyone that your company comes into contact with is like putting a cast on a patient with a broken leg—before you've set the leg.

Believe us: most of our clients come to us thinking they need a new website or email campaign, but when they sit down with us, they usually discover that the work they need to do to reach their goals goes a lot deeper.

When Easton Gastroenterology first hired us, for example, owner Dr. William Moss asked us for traditional marketing services. Like many of our clients, he wanted more leads. He told us he had been successfully advertising his practice via bus ads, billboards, and pay-per-click online ads.

However, while he was getting leads in the door, he was facing a couple of frustrating problems:

- His customer acquisition cost was very high: Easton had a lot of leads who were coming to them who just were not a good fit. As a result, his medical team was wasting a lot of their valuable (and expensive) time evaluating these individuals—only to have to refer them out.

- There were also problems in the process of taking a lead from the first phone call to their initial consultation with Dr. Moss. Too many qualified leads were not making it in to see him.

What's really interesting is that—at first glance—Dr. Moss was in a position many businesses would find enviable. He had figured out an advertising system that got people in the door. He had lots of leads!

Unfortunately, the leads were not making Easton much profit. This is why Dr. Moss came to us—he thought that to make more money, he just needed to ramp up lead generation.

We didn't rule that out, but thought it was important to run an overall assessment of his business. As we began to dive into the Easton ecosystem with Dr. Moss and his team, we found several issues:

- The intake process wasn't systematized: the reception staff had no process for talking with leads and qualifying them based on their presenting symptoms. Dr. Moss's clinic was exceptional at treating certain types of gastroenteric conditions—but too many patients were coming in with other problems that Dr. Moss was less qualified to treat. The high volume of unqualified clients not only wasted the doctor's time, it also frustrated patients and put the company's brand reputation at risk.

- The receptionists also weren't effectively screening potential patients' insurance coverage. In today's complex insurance world, certain insurance plans didn't cover Dr. Moss's practice. People who came in but couldn't get treated due to their type of insurance was—quite understandably—highly frustrating for Dr. Moss, their insurance specialist, staff, and patients.

- The front desk was doing a poor job of scheduling. Instead of stacking appointments so that patients could be seen *sooner*, they were haphazardly filling in Dr. Moss's schedule so that some patients had to wait five to six weeks for their initial appointment! As a result of this long wait, potential patients were cancelling appointments to go elsewhere. In addition, it created gaps in the schedule for both Dr. Moss and his nurses, creating times when Easton was paying people to do paperwork instead of seeing patients.

- Due to the issues with intake, Dr. Moss, his two nurses, and his insurance specialist were irritated with the four people working at the front desk answering phones, processing paperwork, and scheduling appointments. Meanwhile, the front desk staff were bickering with one another and thought the medical team was "pretentious." The staff in each department believed that the staff in the other departments didn't understand them. Drama pervaded the everyday atmosphere at the practice, keeping all of the staff from providing the very best in service.

Instead of working with Dr. Moss on lead generation immediately, we asked him whether he'd ever clearly communicated his mission, values, or vision to his staff.

He seemed surprised by the question. Like many of our clients, he had developed a mission and values when writing his initial business plan, but never went over them with the staff. As for a vision? Well, he was so busy growing the practice, he hadn't had time to think about it.

He couldn't remember his mission exactly, but when he looked it up, this is what he found:

"Improve the health and lives of people through excellent and compassionate care."

Unfortunately, he had never systematized either this mission or his core values into behaviors that could be embodied by every employee. So it followed that the front desk just assumed that someone else would make the call about who was qualified. No one took ownership to solve the problem immediately.

The work ahead became clear. We worked with Dr. Moss and his team to:

- Streamline the lead intake process so that there were fewer unqualified patients getting through the door.

- Shorten the time it takes before a qualified patient gets to see Dr. Moss for an initial evaluation. This almost eliminated gaps in the schedule, saving the practice wasted payroll expenses and converting more leads into patients.

- Systematize screening each lead's insurance to ensure each person had the right coverage.

- Stop the infighting between staff members by creating systems to enforce the mission and values. This made the company a better place for both employees *and* patients, and it worked more efficiently because people weren't wasting time bickering.

Thanks to the internal shifts that Easton made, the company became more profitable as a result of all of the gains in efficiency and increases in both staff and patient satisfaction. They were also able to reduce the money they spent on advertising because they screened leads more carefully, reduced cancellations, and the happier patients referred more new patients to them.

We developed our Marketing From the Inside Out® system because we believe traditional marketing methods are broken—especially for B2B companies. Moreover, we've discovered that even excellent marketing case studies from Fortune 100 companies do not scale down correctly for small- and mid-sized businesses.

In contrast to most marketing approaches, our system targets the core of a company and gravitates outward. We help leaders isolate the true essence of their brand, articulate their remarkability, and integrate their mission, values, and vision into every aspect of their business.

The companies we've worked with have reaped the benefits of creating a powerful internal culture of brand champions who are motivated by performance and purpose. They find it a lot easier to attract right-fit clients and talent who are engaged and loyal. And they've discovered how to view their marketing as a systematic, high-performing machine that builds and sustains relationships with both external *and* internal customers.

While we designed the system with small- to mid-sized B2B businesses in mind, these ideas are applicable for most types of companies—regardless of their size or their industry. Companies selling all types of services—from engineering to medicine to accounting to skilled trades—have embraced this methodology and thrived as the result of it.

If you want to know if applying Marketing From the Inside Out®, is right for you, then you can answer the following questions:

- Do we want to have a great culture with engaged employees?
- Would we like to carve out a company differentiation where we are perceived as the leader in our industry?
- Could a consistent stream of qualified leads who seek *our* company out for our expertise be beneficial?
- Do we want a consistent marketing strategy with systems to consistently implement it?
- Is it right for us to develop a strategic planning process to move our company forward into the future?
- Would our company be more cohesive if we developed strong values and a mission that supports our core purpose?
- Will it improve our culture and customer service if we had a workforce that consists of A players?

The good news is: you likely already have all the knowledge you need to make your company remarkable—one where you and your employees love going to work, and where your customers love doing business with you. You can create a purpose-driven company that gets the results you want and moves you toward achieving a Big Vision.

But first, a word of warning: making your company remarkable by applying our system will be one of the toughest projects you will ever undertake. It takes grit, determination, and consistency.

But the rewards of transforming your company this way are immeasurable. Our clients have experienced increased brand reputation, higher profit margins, decreased employee turnover, bigger account sizes, larger customer lifetime values, steady revenue growth, and waiting lists for their services.

For example, one analytics firm that we worked with implemented Marketing From the Inside Out® and realized a *200 percent growth* in its average customer value.

This was a direct result of their increased focus on hiring the right people who were engaged and motivated to grow the company. Their leadership team's commitment to the mission and values of the organization resulted in amazing customer service, which led to an increased customer spend and greatly improved customer retention, leading to a higher average customer lifetime value.

Another client—a skilled trades company—reinvented their thirty-five-year-old company by applying the Marketing From the Inside Out® systems. They shifted their focus to developing an engaged workforce that championed their brand and lived their values. As a result, they increased their employee retention rate to more than 90 percent and increased their customer acquisition rate by 46 percent. They were also able to move into servicing larger commercial spaces— going head to head with national companies, and winning the bids based on their new brand message and reputation.

Marketing From the Inside Out® will help you realize similar successes by helping you go beyond traditional, superficial marketing tips and, instead, help you build a remarkable company from the inside out. It's challenging work, but our clients have found it to not only be profitable, but deeply fulfilling.

PRINCIPLE #1

START FROM
THE INSIDE

"The ability to make good decisions regarding
people represents one of the last reliable sources
of competitive advantage, since very few
organizations are very good at it."

—Peter Drucker, management consultant and author

What's the secret to bringing in new customers?

THIS WAS THE QUESTION KEEPING DARREN COPPEDGE, THE
CEO of Springfield Collections Agency, up at night. Darren is a
cheery upbeat man always ready with a smile for customers and
employees alike. He joined the debt collection company in his early
twenties, worked his way up to manager, and eventually purchased
the company from the original founder. He now employs thirty-
eight people.

SCA has a stable portfolio of business customers, most of which
have been with them for years. They have a good collections recovery
rate and provide strong customer service.

But Darren was struggling to get new customers.

To start, it was hard to reach the decision-makers at the types of organizations he was targeting (hospitals, property management companies, financial institutions, universities). And since the company has had a history of relying on referrals from existing customers, they had no marketing in place to attract new business.

As a result, the company was experiencing almost stagnant growth with only one or two new clients each quarter. This was a risky position to be in, since it meant that if they lost one of their larger clients, they would face a significant drop in revenue.

When Darren contacted us, he wanted us to create a marketing plan that would help him bring in more qualified leads and develop the funnels that would convert them into customers.

As we started working with Darren to develop his marketing plan, we learned he also faced problems with employee retention. He told us that a lot of the people he hires leave in two years or less. He also struggles with recruiting—he just can't find the talent he needs who can do the job well and will stick around to help his company grow.

But recruitment and retention issues were par for the course in his industry. When it comes right down to it, Darren told us, nobody likes debt collectors. After all, repeated calls from collection agencies can be incredibly traumatizing, especially if you've recently lost a job or you're worried about your credit score. Many people simply do not have the money to repay the companies they owe.

Of course, he continued, it's not too hard to empathize with the person who *owes* the money.

But, he said, think about what it's like for the *collector.*

While occasionally collectors will have pleasant calls with people who are willing to set up payment plans, many debtors reply with excuses as to why they can't pay—and they can be hard to hear. And some of the calls are worse—a lot worse. People will scream, call the collectors names, cry, curse, threaten, and hang up.

Picture doing this all day, every day—and making only fourteen to seventeen dollars an hour doing it. As you can imagine, being a debt collector is an incredibly stressful job. Unsurprisingly, the industry is notorious for having a high turnover rate.

So there was really nothing Darren could do about this, right? He should just accept that high turnover rate goes part and parcel with his industry and double down on his marketing efforts.

Let's take a closer look.

We told Darren that, of course, we could help him with his lead generation issue. But we added that his recruitment and retention problem was not as unfixable as he believed.

Provided he was willing to start from the inside.

More about that in just a moment. But first, let's talk about the existing paradigm and how it results in a phenomenon often called a "leaky bucket."

Many marketing books and agencies focus primarily on reaching external customers: getting leads and—hopefully—nurturing relationships with existing clients. And, of course, this is important. But it is a recipe that is missing a lot of ingredients—in our opinion, it's like baking chocolate chip cookies that are only made from flour and butter.

Because unless you turn to a book on human resources or leadership or hire an agency that is focused on these areas, you won't learn much about engaging and retaining your *other* set of customers: the internal ones. This includes everyone from your leadership team to your managers, frontline workers, interns, and contractors.

A lot of the companies that come to us have a siloed approach: with marketing handling external branding and lead generation, human resources tackling internal employee engagement and recruitment, and any other number of departments focusing on customer service delivery and account management. There is no holistic business ecosystem in play.

We think this is a huge mistake, one that hurts your chances not only to attract and retain the best talent—but also the best customers.

All too often, small- to mid-sized businesses frontload all of their marketing dollars into lead generation. Unfortunately, they don't focus on onboarding a prospect and ensuring their graceful transition to becoming a customer. There is no process for introducing each customer to dedicated employees who are responsible for nurturing the relationship and meeting their needs at every touchpoint. These customers are not regularly acknowledged, helped, thanked, and recognized for their loyalty. The workforce is not encouraged by leadership to be obsessive about delighting customers.

And because there is no internal system for nurturing customers, there is high customer attrition—multiple "one-and-done" projects that result in a short customer life cycle (and as a result—lower profits).

This is the "leaky bucket" phenomena—companies pay a lot of money to acquire a customer, but then because they don't nurture the relationship and work to provide more value over time, the customer drifts away. There is little brand loyalty and few word-of-mouth referrals.

What's more, this same phenomenon plays out with an organization's workforce. When companies hire employees, they often put a lot of money into advertising the position and allocate staff time to interviewing candidates. But after they hire someone and provide some basic training, the employee is set adrift, without a lot of guidance from leadership. The newly hired person is not formally oriented into a nurturing culture that emphasizes and measures specific performance goals.

As a result of being left to their own devices, employees lack motivation and a sense of overall purpose. They are never told how their day-to-day work connects to the larger vision of the organization. In addition, no one at the organization is spending time with employees to learn what motivates and satisfies them. This leads to poor performances, disengagement, and high turnover rates.

When employees feel unsatisfied and disengaged, they don't go the extra mile for your company. And, they certainly aren't bending over backwards to delight your customers.

Think about the impact your employees are having on the success of your company. Every day, your employees interact with customers, prospects, and potential referrers on the phone. They can communicate with them at meetings, in the halls, via email, and on social media. When they're done for the day, they go to stores, restaurants, gyms, banks, and bars and they talk about your company. They call, text, post, comment, upload, and Skype—and you better believe they're talking about where they work.

More than ever, your employees have a huge array of ways to communicate to the world about your company.

And with all of that interaction, you gotta wonder . . .

When your employees talk about your company, are they saying good things? When they speak to your customers, prospects, and networks, are they reflecting a positive company image? Are they helping to bring in more dream customers who will help your company grow? Do they work to bring in new awesome employees? Do they bend over backwards to deliver remarkable service to your customers?

In other words, do your employees act as committed, passionate ambassadors for your brand? Do they have a good grasp of what your brand really represents?

If they're not, ask yourself: what would it be like if your employees—all of them—were an active part of your marketing and sales team? What if they were continuously working to share the value of all of your products and services to your customers, working to cross-sell and up-sell? Not in a pushy way—but because they so believe in your products or services that they can't help but talk passionately about them?

Most of all, what would it be like if your employees were really, truly engaged, motivated, satisfied, and wholeheartedly committed to the ongoing success of your company? What if they lived and breathed your company's mission and values?

So how do you do it?

You intentionally build a cohesive culture that is driven to live and breathe your company values, rally around its mission, and move it forward toward your Big Vision. You ensure that you have systems and processes in place to plug the leaky bucket and instead work hard to keep employees and customers so engaged that they will stay with your organization for the long haul.

Improved Employee Engagement

Better Service, Employee Retention, Productivity

Higher Customer Satisfaction and Brand Loyalty

More Revenue and Profit

ENGAGEMENT: THE SECRET WEAPON
FOR BUILDING A STRONG BRAND

WE'VE SEEN POWERFUL RESULTS WHEN OUR CLIENTS start thinking deliberately about building a culture where every employee is truly engaged—where they feel a deep connection to the work they're doing and the goods and services they're providing.

We begin by helping leaders identify their mission, vision, and values, and then walk them through the process of weaving these core ideas into their operations.

Earlier in the chapter, we talked about the challenges Darren faced at his debt collection agency, Springfield Collection Agency (SCA). We told him that by starting from the inside, he could solve both his lead issue and his talent problem. While skeptical at first, Darren trusted our process.

One of the first things we did was to take him through our processes of crafting his One-Word Mission™ and his Living, Breathing Values™.

Darren told us he believes that debt recovery starts with respect and integrity and realized that SCA could be doing more to make his belief "respect people" a Living, Breathing Value™. We set up goals around exceeding client expectations and also came up with a plan for being a more engaged member of their local community: for instance, volunteering for charitable causes.

Next, we helped SCA's leadership team develop a strategy to weave the value "respect people" into their systems: that meant revising job descriptions, hiring processes, employee goals setting, and performance evaluations. We also led a series of facilitated meetings where leadership brainstormed ways to make SCA a more fun and exciting place to work. The leaders also came up with systems to hold their direct reports accountable to living the mission and values.

One idea that emerged from these sessions involved gamifying the work that the collectors were doing. These friendly competitions capitalized on the spirit of the new mission and values by incentivizing people to push further with their collection efforts in a respectful manner. For example, when an account representative could get a debtor on an automatic payment plan or get them to increase their monthly payment by 10 percent, the collector would get special chips. The SCA employees could then save these chips and use them at an auction at the end-of-the-year party to bid on items such as gift certificates and iPads.

Another practice that we put into place was to find champions within the organization who helped organize philanthropic teams to participate in multiple employee-chosen causes that aligned with the company's value of "be a good neighbor." This not only helped boost the morale by giving back to the local community, but it also helped boost SCA's visibility in events such as walk-a-thons where potential clients had walking teams as well.

We also developed a system wherein any time an employee accomplished a performance goal or received a testimonial aligned with a company value, this achievement would be broadcast high up on the wall of the company's call center.

Next we worked with SCA to transform their hiring process. We first wove their mission and values into their job descriptions. Then, we designed an online career center that emphasized hiring A players and allowed Darren to "build his bench" even when he wasn't actively bringing people on board.

We then created a careful hiring process that only allowed people into the organization who aligned with its mission and values. As part of orientation, Darren would personally sit down with each new hire and tell them about his beliefs and convictions about the mission and values. Finally we helped SCA redesign their employee goal setting and performance reviews to reflect the organization's mission and values.

By over-communicating his mission and values to his team and creating a more supportive culture, Darren changed the dynamics at his company. Both the long-term SCA employees and the new hires learned to embrace the concept that the job of debt collector had meaning and purpose.

By starting from the inside, SCA significantly reduced their staff turnover rate. Because SCA was making wiser hiring decisions, they were finding people who stayed on longer. They began to attract talent who were excited to work there and committed to the company's mission and values.

While all of the internal work was going on, we also worked on creating a new visual identity for the company with a website and marketing materials that expressed their mission and values. We helped SCA put new sales and marketing processes into place. The company increased their client portfolio but they also gained clarity about the kinds of clients they were looking for.

SCA not only increased their revenue and their profitability, but a manager told us that one of their newest hires said on her first day, "I've never been around so many friendly employees in my life!"

SCA is an incredible example of the power of employee engagement. But we are not the only ones to have discovered what motivated and inspired employees can do for a company. In fact, multiple studies have revealed the impact of an engaged workforce.

In an ongoing multi-year study of more than twenty-five million employees across geographies and industries, Gallup found that business units that ranked in the top 25 percent of their organizations for employee engagement showed:

- 22 percent higher profitability
- 21 percent higher productivity
- 10 percent higher customer satisfaction
- 37 percent lower absenteeism
- 48 percent fewer safety incidents
- 41 percent fewer quality incidents (defects)

Astonishing, right?

Few of today's most successful leaders would argue against the importance of focusing on building a culture where employee engagement is fostered and rewarded. According to Ginni Rometty, CEO of IBM, "Culture is your company's number one asset." And Starbucks Corporation founder and former CEO Howard Schultz has written that "so much of what Starbucks achieved was because of [its employees] and the culture they fostered."

Not surprisingly, most Fortune 100 companies "get" culture and they spend a lot of time and energy making big investments in it.

And yet, culture is something most small- to mid-sized companies tend to ignore.

Why?

1. **It takes a lot of work around soft skills executives tend to devalue.** As a leader, you may not consciously overlook the impact of an engaged workforce. It's just hard to make the case for prioritizing something so seemingly intangible when you're focused on the nose-to-the-wheel daily grind. Many leaders don't understand that focusing on the soft stuff can have a powerful impact on the bottom line—but in our experience, it can, and does.

2. **Building a great culture takes time—and it's time you can't bill for.** When you are in fast-growth mode, time is a precious resource, and there's always too much work to be done. We understand—going from the three-inch, in-the-weeds view to the twenty-thousand-foot strategic perspective of your company is hard. Small businesses especially need to work hard to bring in revenue by focusing on billable work and every minute spent thinking about long-term strategy can feel like money wasted.

    But in our experience, focusing on the engagement of your employees and creating a purpose-driven, values-oriented culture can result in higher per-hour input than any billable activity you take on.

    And there is evidence to back this up: In their book *Corporate Culture and Performance*, John Kotter and James Heskett show that over a decade-long period, purposeful, value-driven companies outperform their counterparts in stock price by a factor of twelve.

    In addition, *The Towers Watson 2012 Global Workforce Study* of thirty-two thousand employees in more than a thousand businesses found that those companies with the highest engagement had an operating margin of 27 percent, while those at the lowest engagement levels were less than 10 percent.

3. **Employee engagement is hard to measure as a stand-alone metric.** It's not difficult to measure work in terms of time invoiced, widgets produced, or services sold. But it's a lot harder to measure employee engagement.

    The good news is that there are hard engagement metrics that you can start to use in your key performance indicators (KPIs). You can measure indicators such as employee retention and turnover, improved customer retention, increased productivity, reduced absenteeism, extra hours worked per salaried employee, percentage of employees meeting performance goals, and so on.

If you're still having doubts about what would happen if you turned your focus to employee engagement, consider what Alcoa Power and Propulsion was able to accomplish by setting their sights on something so seemingly "soft." After a period of business downturn and leadership changes, employee engagement dropped significantly as evidenced by surveys the company collected from its workforce.

As a result, management took on a commitment to rebuild itself as "an employer of choice." The leadership team made dedicated efforts toward improving a variety of areas including well-being initiatives, increased transparency, and heightened communication with employees. The business results are impressive. Staff turnover reduced from 22 percent in 2010 to less than 1 percent in 2013; on-time delivery increased from 46.7 percent in 2009 to 96 percent; and labor productivity is increasing by 10 percent year on year, testament to the employee engagement profit chain in action.[9]

THE DANGERS OF DISENGAGEMENT

AS A LEADER, YOU HAVE AN OPPORTUNITY TO CREATE THE kind of culture and work environment that energizes your employees. If people feel like their company cares about supporting them and their families, believe us, they're going to talk about it.

But there's perhaps an even more urgent reason to start building a culture of engagement at your organization—one that you ignore at your peril.

The Gallup poll we mentioned earlier also revealed that a whopping 70 percent of the American workforce is not reaching their full potential. Of these, about 50 percent fall into a category that Gallup calls "Not Engaged." These folks are emotionally disconnected, checked out, and less likely to be productive. They are essentially sleepwalking through their day. As a result, an organization's vital economic influencers—their ability to grow and innovate—are at high risk.

The other 20 percent are "Actively Disengaged" in their work. These are the folks that you need to avoid hiring or must move off your payroll (yes, this means you will have to let them go).

Not only are these employees acting out their unhappiness and actually working to undermine what their company accomplishes, a growing body of research suggests that having even a few unengaged employees can quickly turn a positive working environment into a divisive and negative atmosphere. These "bad apples" have the power to ruin the performance of a team or an entire organization—no matter how stellar the other employees.

We point this out because as you begin to build a great company culture full of engaged employees, you are going to have to make some really hard decisions about certain people on your team.

And let us say it again: you are going to have to either put them in a different position in your company or—more likely—you are going to have to let them go.

We can't stress this point enough. Poor performers not only under-deliver; they also bring others down with them. In the 2006 study *How, When, and Why Bad Apples Spoil the Barrel*, University of New South Wales Professor Will Felps and his colleagues discovered that just one "bad apple" will drive down team effectiveness by 30 to 40 percent.

Even though we want to believe that a strong, high-performing team can overcome the one bad apple, test after test shows that there's simply no winning with a losing player.

In the history of our company, we weren't as adept at hiring A players and hired our share of bad apples. In one instance, there was one employee who—unbeknownst to us—was bringing his own computer and cell phone to our office and using these to take on freelance assignments for his own clients during working hours. It goes without saying that his productivity wasn't what it should've been.

But the bigger cost was that our other employees saw what he was doing and it began to poison the team dynamic. They couldn't understand how he was getting away with it and they felt justifiably angry about what he was doing. This hurt their productivity and prevented them from feeling motivated or enthusiastic about their work.

Ultimately, we became aware of this person's disengagement and let him go. Unsurprisingly, our team's morale and production went up. People were more focused, reported being more satisfied, and we watched our revenues climb to new heights . . . even with one fewer person on our small team!

BAD APPLES IN YOUR BUSINESS

YOU, TOO, MAY HAVE ONE OR MORE OF THESE BAD APPLES on your team. Be honest with yourself—you probably already know who they are and why they aren't performing at the level you expect. While letting someone go is never easy, we've never had a client tell us "Wow, I really fired that person too fast!" Instead, it was usually long overdue. When you move these people out of your organization, you make room for people who are enthusiastic and committed, and you allow the rest of your team to live up to their full potential each and every day. (And if you're still finding it hard to let a bad apple go, keep in mind that doing so makes it possible for that person to own up to his or her behavior or find a company that's a better fit.)

HOW ENGAGEMENT TIES INTO
YOUR COMPANY CULTURE

HIGH LEVELS OF EMPLOYEE ENGAGEMENT ARE AN OUTCOME of a healthy, positive organizational culture. And, ultimately, a healthy culture is one where employees are excited and motivated to work there, and they perform to their highest potential.

At its most basic level, a culture is "the way things work around here." Culture is the invisible force that guides beliefs, values, social norms, office rituals, and common practices that your entire company shares in common—from CEO to intern. A great culture is one in which employees thrive and everyone involved is engaged, motivated, and fulfilled. People in a great culture are helping one another to be great. They support everyone in achieving the highest performance possible.

Let's be clear—your company has a culture whether you planned it or not. Unfortunately, unplanned cultures are often rife with drama, bad apples, and unhappiness. And, at the extreme end, there are cultures that are downright toxic and can cause employees to have high anxiety, insomnia, loss of motivation, dread of work, and a whole host of other physical symptoms.

At its very worst, there are cultures like the one at Wells Fargo where the overwhelming majority of employees learned to push the boundaries of ethical behavior in order to get bonus compensation. Leaders at Wells Fargo were all highly compensated for hitting performance targets, which lead to not only their acceptance of unethical behaviors in their direct reports, but were actually reinforcing and coaching it.

Federal regulators said Wells Fargo employees secretly created millions of unauthorized bank and credit card accounts—without customers knowing it—since 2011. And customers were charged fees on these ghost accounts. More than 5,300 employees were terminated and Wells Fargo was hit with $185 million in fines and an additional $5 million in refunds to its customers.

Former employees of Wells Fargo said the toxic high-pressure sales culture at the bank drove some workers to deceive customers and open unauthorized accounts—even in the bank's own headquarters building in San Francisco.

In an interview with National Public Radio (NPR), one employee described the sales pressure this way: "It was every day, man. It was literally every day. It was a grind-house."

Mornings began with a huddle with managers pressing workers to meet their "solutions goals"—in other words, selling more products such as home equity loans or credit cards.

"It was multiple occasions where I saw my coworkers were cracking under the pressure," he said. "Tears, crying, constantly getting pulled into the back room having one-on-ones for coaching sessions."

Of course, these so-called coaching sessions were really just sessions where employees were pushed to sell more "solutions." The employee likened working there to being in an abusive relationship.

Another employee said after one of these coaching sessions she threw up in the wastebasket under her desk. "You were stuck and it was the feeling that no other employer is going to want you because we will ruin you," she said.[10]

Of course, this is an extreme example of a toxic culture, but it does demonstrate the profound effect that the culture of an organization has on shaping the behaviors of its employees. And while we hope your culture looks nothing like Wells Fargo's, you could still be suffering from high turnover and low productivity because you haven't focused on creating an amazing culture that fosters a sense of satisfaction and belonging.

We won't lie—changing an entrenched culture is challenging. It starts with someone on your leadership team making the initial decision that a healthy, positive culture is a priority. Then, you begin to treat your employees as your frontline internal customers who you serve.

This book will take you step by step through actions that you can take to transform your workplace into one where employees thrive and everyone involved is engaged, motivated, and fulfilled. Before we dive too deeply into our Marketing From the Inside Out® methodology, we wanted to highlight some of what we've found to be the key elements of a great culture:

THE SECRETS TO CREATING A GREAT CULTURE

1. **Attract, hire, and retain highly engaged, A players who are aligned with the company's mission, values, and vision.** In his book, *Topgrading*, Bradford Smart defines an A player as "one who qualifies among the top 10 percent of those available for a position. An A player is 'best of class.'" These are the individuals who can motivate a team and bring their maximum effort every day. They actively wish to see the company succeed, and their attitude is contagious—these individuals can inspire a culture of performance. The more of them you have, the better your results.

2. **Onboard employees with passion in order to show them how important they are to your company.** Set up your new hire for

success by having an intentional onboarding and orientation process that teaches them your mission, vision, and values from day one.

The Ritz-Carlton has this down to a fine science. New hires at The Ritz-Carlton spend most of their two-day onboarding learning about the company's culture, values, and credo. The new staff is introduced to the culture through videos, presentations by managers, and group discussions.

"If you waste the first few hours discussing anything other than values, you're wasting your opportunity," said Diana Oreck, former vice president of The Ritz-Carlton Leadership Center.

But the work doesn't stop there.

"Your culture must be enlivened every day," said Oreck. "It's not enough to talk about your organizational culture when your profit and loss statement (P&L) has gone south. You must find a way for your culture to go from employees' heads to their hearts. When they internalize the culture they then 'live' the culture consistently."

3. **Reinforce and reward employees for living your mission and values.** There are many ways to celebrate success at all levels—company, departmental, and individual. Tie rewards in to your mission and values so that your team is continuously reminded of their impact. Have fun and be creative with celebrations. One of our clients has an annual event where employees play sports like flag football and soccer. The teams are named for each of their four values—this is a silly, yet endearing way for the workforce to be reminded of the values.

At Kinesis, at each of our monthly all-team meetings, we save five to ten minutes at the end for team members to "Share the Good," which is one of our values. Employees go around and recognize another employee who was especially helpful to them that month. We also send Share the Good emails to let everyone know when someone on the team has gone above and beyond for a client.

4. **Grow strong leaders from within your company who believe in radical transparency and authentic communication.** These employees not only evangelize the company's mission, vision, and values but live them by example.

5. **Tie employee and company goals and performance to mission, vision, and values.** This will build a stronger brand and culture over time and help remind your team of your leadership's commitment and passion for your mission, vision, and values.

6. **Be obsessive about delighting your customers.** Produce, design, develop, invent, and innovate with your customer in mind. Always focus on the things you can do to create value and success for your customers. They are an integral part of your culture.

7. **Live your values in bad times, as well as good.** If you are truly living and breathing your core values, then you must stand by them regardless of what comes your way. In 2008, Maple Leaf Food was implicated in a foodborne illness caused by an outbreak of Listeria. One of the company's values is "Do What's Right: By acting with integrity, behaving responsibly, and treating people with respect." In response to the crisis, CEO Michael McCain immediately took responsibility with a post to the public on their website and on video: "Certainly knowing that there is a desire to assign blame, I want to reiterate that the buck stops right here . . . our best efforts failed, not the regulators or the Canadian

food safety system . . . I emphasize: this is our accountability and it's ours to fix, which we are taking on fully."[11]

He then went on to recall all 220 packaged meats from the plant, which cost the company millions and millions of dollars, but kept more people from getting sick and/or dying. By 2010, the company's overall meat revenues had recovered 95 percent of their former value.[12]

8. **Work with customers who are in alignment with your values and mission.** Cherry-pick your dream customers by getting really clear on who you want to service. Communicate this through both your marketing collateral and your sales team. By selecting these right-fit customers, you create a more positive experience for your entire team, furthering their motivation to be engaged and provide the absolute best service.

You might think: this *sounds* good—but also a little overwhelming. Where do I start? Don't worry—we'll be expanding on all these ideas in the next several chapters. Building a great culture starts with your One-Word Mission™, so that's where we'll go next.

YOUR MISSION IS THE HEART OF YOUR BUSINESS

"Don't ever take a job—join a crusade!
Find a cause that you can believe in and
give yourself to it completely."

—Colleen Barrett, retired president of Southwest Airlines

IF YOU ASK MOST DOCTORS TO NAME THEIR BIGGEST challenges, you probably don't expect to hear "making the beds" at the top of the list. And yet, that was exactly the problem threatening the viability of the culture at Dr. Robert Jones's clinic.

Dr. Jones owns a sleep medicine clinic that specializes in treating people who suffer from sleep apnea. To properly diagnose this disorder, a patient is required to undergo a sleep study in the clinic. Because this small practice consists of only twelve team members, the daily responsibilities of stripping the sheets and making the beds falls upon the front-desk staff.

Very unglamorous.

For years, Dr. Jones struggled with people in this position who resented this particular duty. And, rightfully so—making beds is typically not something that an administrative person has to take on. But the company was not big enough nor did they have enough sleep-study rooms to justify hiring a person who was dedicated solely to tidying and making beds. As a result, the beds were often not made with the attention and diligence that Dr. Jones would have liked to see.

The administrative person's reluctance affected the rest of the staff, causing resentment between other team members.

After our initial discussion with Dr. Jones, the problem became very clear to us. He'd never properly defined or articulated his core mission to his employees—nor had he explained to his staff why the seemingly small task of making the bed was so vital to carrying out that mission.

We'll return to what Dr. Jones did next in a moment—but first, let's dive deep into why failure to articulate a mission is such a common problem.

Whenever we work with new clients, one of our first conversations centers around asking each company's leaders to tell us a bit about their mission. Frequently we find that founders need to go searching for this information—sometimes it's hidden somewhere on the website, if it's there at all. More often, the small- to medium-sized business owners we work with need to go rooting through a pile of paperwork or digital archives they haven't glanced at since they opened shop.

The reasons behind this phenomenon are understandable.

In the early days of a company, founders often spend time

drafting, wordsmithing, and editing several different distillations of their mission statements (some authors and researchers call it a "core purpose"—we will use the two terms interchangeably). These may include value propositions, vision proclamations, or mission statements, depending on what system their approach is based on.

Often mission statements are required as part of a business plan they created to help raise start-up capital. Or the leadership wrote a mission because they heard they needed to do so in order to get their company going.

Unfortunately, all too often, this initial flurry of writing languishes on a shelf (or in a digital folder); this visioning work has already been checked off a list, and these important efforts are frequently forgotten before the metaphorical ink has dried.

But when leadership can't even remember their missions, you can bet these tenets certainly aren't helping to engage employees in their day-to-day activities. Moreover, most mission statements are neither inspiring nor memorable—they feature overly long and wordy paragraphs, filled with platitudes. They hang on a wall in a gold frame or are plastered on a website page, but no one ever reads them.

Throughout the rest of this chapter and book, we are going to show you how to create and integrate a memorable and meaningful mission within your company.

But first, why is this so important?

People have a fundamental need to know that what they are doing serves a greater purpose—that they're making a difference and working toward something greater than "the daily grind." A clear mission helps employees at every level of your company feel more engaged and satisfied—it reminds them that there's a reason they come to work every day.

Consider this—we spend a large amount of each week at our

workplace, so as employers, we have a real opportunity to help our staff see how they are connected to a greater purpose. In fact, in her books on work and culture, Margaret Heffernan has written that research shows the happiest people aren't those with the most money but those with *purpose*—a sense that they are contributing to something bigger than themselves.[13]

Unfortunately—as we explored in the last chapter—the majority of people are not engaged in their work. Instead, they view work as a means to an end—suffering through Mondays and Hump Days and thanking God that it's Friday so that they can spend the weekends on the things that do give their lives meaning: family, friends, faith, hobbies, vacations, and so on. What's more, as we mentioned earlier, many companies are focused on maximizing shareholder value instead of trying to make their workplaces a good place to work.

Consider your own company, people, and culture for a moment: If your workforce is not driven by its mission, then you have a tremendous opportunity on your hands.

In fact, a three-year survey commissioned by Deloitte found that focusing on purpose rather than profits builds business confidence and drives investment. Organizations that instill a culture of purpose are more likely to find long-term success.[14]

"There is a clear connection between a sense of purpose that delivers positive impacts for all stakeholders and sustained business success," explains Punit Renjen, CEO of Deloitte. "Furthermore, leaders need to articulate a culture of purpose—and, equally important, serve as a visible, consistent example of those behaviors. That's a terrific blueprint for any organization that wants to become and remain exceptional."

In our work, we've found that organizations without a driving mission operate in a largely reactive manner—leadership and employees run around putting out fires instead of proactively fire-proofing their companies. Teams get lost in a variety of projects, pursuits, and "great" ideas that do not fit together and often don't even get completed.

In contrast, company leaders with a shared core purpose know what fuels and guides their strategies and goals. A clear mission allows you to build a thriving culture, set the right direction for new products and services, and attract the best employees and customers. It provides a road map to ensure everyone in your organization stays on track.

In a 2013 study of 49,928 business units across 192 organizations representing forty-nine different industries in thirty-four countries, Gallup researchers found that a company's mission is a powerful driver of organizational performance.[15] They identified five factors behind the success-promoting, margin-boosting benefits of focusing on mission:

1. **Mission drives loyalty across generations.** Emphasizing mission and purpose are two of the strongest factors for retaining Millennials, Generation Xers, *and* Boomers.

2. **Mission fosters customer engagement.** Only about 41 percent of employees know what makes their organization's brand different from competitors. A strong mission promotes brand differentiation and engagement and customer loyalty.

3. **Mission improves strategic alignment.** Your mission establishes and balances priorities and sets performance goals. You should hire and promote people based on their ability to deliver on the promise of your mission.

4. **Mission brings clarity.** When your leadership and employees know your mission, it helps them make decisions and determine priorities.

5. **Mission can be measured.** In a mission-driven culture, leaders can evaluate employee engagement through surveys and other assessments. Managers can use this feedback to help employees see how their work connects to the company's mission.

There's another important reason for clearly articulating your mission. Roy Spence, coauthor of *It's Not What You Sell, It's What You Stand For* calls purpose a crucial strategic structure that pulls companies through the worst of times. It simplifies many difficult decisions and makes an uncertain future easier to navigate.

"Organizations that have a clear purpose," he writes, "won't be looking for silver bullets or grasping at straws or just cutting cost with no clear focus. Instead, they will have more clarity in their cuts and more certainty on how to stimulate revenues."

Before we examine the way in which a mission can be meaningful for small- and mid-size businesses, we'd like to zoom to the big dogs for a moment—those Fortune 500 companies and large organizations that have withstood the test of time. They have something to teach us about the importance of clearly articulating a core purpose and making sure employees at every level of the organization understand that what they do matters.

In 1969, during a press briefing in the NASA command center in Houston, Texas, a group of reporters noticed a janitor walking toward them broom in hand, and figured, why not get some B-roll video footage for filler while they were waiting to talk to key officials?

Microphone and camera ready, a reporter asked the janitor, "So what's your job at NASA?" The janitor looked straight at the camera and said, "It's my job to help put a man on the moon."

We learned about this story from Deloitte's 2014 study of organizations with a highly engaged workforce. The researchers found that these companies each possessed a core purpose that went beyond financial or operational objectives. Rather, their mission statements emphasized that each person plays a role in creating value for the entire business's ecosystem.

Leaders at NASA recognize that it is essential to the agency's progress to have an active and deep culture of engagement: every person at NASA knows that they are contributing to a greater purpose. Unsurprisingly, as of this writing, NASA has ranked number one in Best Places to Work in the Federal Government® for five years in a row and counting.[16]

When writing their classic text on organizational success, *Built to Last*, Jim Collins and Jerry Poras embarked upon a six-year study of companies that have prospered over the long term—companies like Hewlett-Packard, 3M, Motorola, Procter & Gamble, Merck, Nordstrom, Sony, Disney, and Marriott. With an average age of one hundred years, the stock of these organizations has performed *fifteen times better* than the overall stock market has since 1926.

Pretty great role models.

By studying companies that have thrived over a sustained period of time, Collins and Poras were able to uncover some key components that have allowed these businesses to both endure and thrive. One of these core elements is a deeply held core purpose or mission that gives the organization a strong sense of identity and continuity.

"An effective purpose reflects the importance people attach to the company's work," they write. "It taps their idealistic motivations—and gets at the deeper reasons for an organization's existence beyond just making money."

Collins and Poras argue this core purpose goes beyond any charismatic leader, product, service, team, or technology. It's the idea of who you are as a company and *why* you exist. As such, an organization's mission has to be completely idealistic. Because at every level of business, from Fortune 500 on down, your ability to prosper as a company is not about what you sell, it's about what each and every employee believes.

Your team knows that their day-to-day activities lead to tangible, tactical results. But when they see exactly how their daily work contributes to a bigger mission, they will be more driven to show up every day on time and do their job well.

Now, you may argue that it's only natural that every employee at NASA or Disney would be inspired by the work the organization does. What about an industry that inspires a bit less wonder than interstellar travel or theatrical fantasy?

MEANING IN CALL CENTERS

LET'S FACE IT—CALL CENTER EMPLOYEES HAVE A TOUGH job. They face repeated 99 percent rejection rates, low pay, and high turnover rate (400 percent, according to Wharton management professor Adam Grant). As a result, morale tends to be quite low. While studying the industry, Professor Grant reported finding a disheartening sign on one employee's desk that read:

> "Doing a good job here is like
> wetting your pants in a dark suit.
> You get a warm feeling, but no one else notices."

Grant has devoted much of his professional career to examining what motivates workers in a variety of industries and settings. He has repeatedly found that employees who know how their work has a meaningful, positive impact on others are not just happier than those who don't, they are also vastly more productive.

In one of his studies from 2007, he obtained permission to talk to the employees of a university call center. Their job was to phone potential donors and ask them to give money to help provide scholarships for students who needed financial assistance. A good cause, for sure, but asking for money is never a fun task, and the staff members were not a highly engaged group who were feeling a strong sense of purpose.

So here's what Grant did. He divided the employees into two groups—the first took part in short chats with the scholarship students about their studies. The second group had no exposure to the donor recipients.

Grant had doubts about his experiment:

I was pretty sure this wasn't going to do a lot of good, because the job itself was still really unpleasant and really stressful," he said. "But I had an inkling of hope that by seeing the scholarship student, the callers would come face to face with someone who really appreciated and valued the work they did. It would show them how their work was making a difference. It would motivate them to work smarter, harder, longer, and to ultimately bring in more money.

Over the month following the callers' meetings with the scholarship recipient, the call center monitored the amount of time workers in the two groups spent on the phone and the amount of money they brought in—and the results were shocking. Grant was so stunned

43

that he replicated the study six more times—but each time got the same result:

> The callers who had interacted with the scholarship recipients spent more than *twice* as much time on the phone as those workers who had not. What's more, they brought in a weekly average *five times* that of the callers who had not interacted with the scholarship student—the typical caller went from $400/week to more than $2,000/week!

And that's just from adding a little bit of meaning to these workers' daily lives. Imagine the impact *you* could make on your employees if you helped them see the connection between their work and your organization's mission!

Once again, we realize it's possible to brush this study aside by pointing out that this organization, too, had a pretty noble purpose—fundraising call centers might not be at the top of many people's lists for ideal jobs, but helping a student is pretty special. But Grant applied the same ideas when studying the training given to seventy-one new call center employees of a Midwestern software firm.

They were selling a good product, but certainly not one likely to pull any heartstrings. So here's how Grant devised a way to add meaning to their calling activities. During their initial training, one group of these trainees got to meet an internal customer—the employees of another department whose salary depends on the sales that the call center makes. Next the CEO met with the callers and explained to them that their work made a difference by supporting other people in the company. By making this connection to the bigger picture—the impact that their calls were having on *others* in the company—the callers' performance improved. And not just by a little—the group realized a significant improvement of *20 percent more revenue per shift.*

This is what happens when you give people a *why,* effectively helping them become more engaged in their work.

Your mission can do the same thing.

When you create a mission and continuously communicate it, weaving it into the everyday fabric of your culture, then amazing things begin to happen:

You'll see an increased sense of commitment in your organization from your staff. Your employees will stop living for the weekend and instead have a bigger purpose that answers the questions, "Why do I come to work each day?" and "Why am I doing this particular task?" And, finally, your leaders and employees will have a compass to help them make decisions about the direction of your business.

YOUR COMPANY'S ONE-WORD MISSION™

NO MATTER WHAT YOUR ORGANIZATION'S SIZE OR SECTOR, you have a core purpose: the work each of your employees does has an impact on the lives of both your internal and external customers. This is your reason for being—your central mission. It can serve to provide meaning and inspiration to your team.

Of course, the challenge for you is to articulate this in a way that helps your employees to get out of bed in the morning with a sense of purpose, to approach even their most menial duties with clarity and focus. The power of a good mission statement cannot be underestimated.

When we think of mission statements that move us, we turn to one of the most successful American companies: Nike.

Their core purpose?

To bring inspiration and innovation to every athlete in the world.

Now that's a mission with meaning—it inspires, it defines the company's reason for being, and it's easy to remember. We love it.

But most companies, from huge corporations to small businesses, just do not get their mission right. Their people do not know their mission—often because it is not succinct or meaningful. Here's an example of a hollow, uninspiring mission statement from a well-known company:

"We are committed to being the world's premier _____ company. To that end, we must continuously achieve superior financial and operating results while adhering to the highest standards of business conduct. These unwavering expectations provide the foundation for our commitments to those with whom we interact."

Can you guess which company this is? It's a major corporation with more than eighty-five thousand employees. Replace the blank line with "petroleum and petrochemical" and you have Exxon's mission statement.

In our opinion, Exxon is getting it completely wrong. We doubt that anyone at the company remembers the mission and we cannot help but question whether it provides any meaning, motivation, or purpose to the thousands of employees who work there.

Exxon—now ExxonMobil—is notorious for having a conservative and secretive culture. Author Steve Coll interviewed more than four hundred present and past employees of Exxon to write his book, *Private Empire: ExxonMobil and American Power.* He writes:

Almost since its founding, the company has emphasized procedure and orthodoxy. But after the wreck [Valdez], Exxon's executives placed extraordinary emphasis on uniform, scientific, idiot-proof, automated systems of safety, management, finance, and business analysis. . . .

The atmosphere within ExxonMobil's offices is one of studied formality; the corporate aesthetic suggests a Four Seasons hotel without many guests. At industry meetings, the ExxonMobil participants can usually be identified easily: the women in charcoal pant suits and the men in dark suits and white shirts, with short and proper haircuts.[17]

ExxonMobil's mission does not seem to be creating a culture that inspires and uplifts people. While they are one of the most profitable companies ever to exist, ExxonMobil is also the only company ever to receive a *negative score* on the Human Rights Campaign's Corporate Equality Index, which rates companies based on their lesbian, gay, bisexual, and transgender (LGBT)-inclusive policies and practices. Shareholders of the petroleum giant have continually rejected an antidiscrimination resolution that would have protected employees from being fired or harassed simply because they are LGBT.[18]

Exxon proves itself to be a loyal adherent to providing the maximum value to its shareholder, and they certainly uphold their mission of "achieving superior financial results." However—as we covered earlier—there is a different way of running a company that supports *all* stakeholders and still brings in revenue and profits.

In our experience, the reward that comes from clearly articulating your mission cannot be underestimated. But—unlike the course that Exxon has followed—we advocate a mission that is inspiring and motivating—one that leaders can evangelize within their company to truly drive people to reach their best potential.

Let's return to the story about Dr. Jones, the owner of the sleep clinic, to demonstrate how. We led him though a planning session, charging him with identifying the "key differentiators" of his business and boiling them down to a concept we've developed at Kinesis—a "One-Word Mission™."

A major differentiator, he realized, was that his practice provided "five-star sleep medicine." Instead of the clinical, lab-like sleep-study rooms of some medical clinics, the entire facility was decorated like a high-end hotel. His research didn't require a lab-like atmosphere so why not make it a beautiful and enjoyable experience?

By looking closely at this unique service he offered, he was able to distill his key differentiators into a One-Word Mission™:

Elegance.

From there, he began to identify core values that supported this philosophy—including "provide five-star customer service." (We'll go deeper into the process of identifying your values in Principle 3.)

Over the next few months, Dr. Jones began to talk about his core mission and values with new hires, at weekly staff meetings, at one-on-one goal-setting meetings and performance reviews, and so on. He even asked Kinesis to create cards with his mission and values, which he gave to every employee for their wallet or purse. As a result of these efforts, his long-standing problems with the front-desk position evaporated.

Once Dr. Jones began to evangelize the mission and values of the organization and explain how all employees in the company served their patients, the front desk person discovered a much deeper meaning behind the menial duty of making the beds. It now made sense why having a crisply made bed with hospital corners and fluffed-up pillows mattered—these seemingly small details supported the overall health of the organization. All of a sudden, bed-making had significance.

What had been a chore that the receptionist considered beneath his skills was transformed into a source of pride. It answered his question, "Why does this matter?" The employee became more engaged and motivated to live the company's mission and values.

HOW TO DEVELOP YOUR MISSION

"People want to believe that they're part of
something meaningful. The sense of purpose
doesn't have to be grandiose or revolutionary,
merely credible and anchored in values."

—Margaret Heffernan, "Another day, another mountain to
climb," fastcompany.com (March 2005)

Now let's talk about your company's core mission.

AT THIS POINT, TAKE A MOMENT TO REFLECT ON YOUR ENTERPRISE,
people, and culture.

Off the top of your head, what's your company's mission? Don't
cheat, don't look at what you may have written down in the past. If
you've already done this work in the past, do your best to remember
what you've identified as your core mission.

Now take a moment and write down what you came up with.
Even if you don't know it verbatim, try to summarize it as best as you
can on paper. Once you've written it down, take a look at your actual
mission statement to see how close you came to getting it right. (If you
don't have a mission statement for your company, don't worry. You
don't need to already have one to apply the lessons in this chapter.)

Sadly, most of us don't know our company's mission. We can't
easily recite it. Even when we are the ones who wrote it! But if you
aren't using it on a daily basis inside your company, you can be absolutely sure that your employees don't know it either.

From our perspective, a mission should:

- Be easy to remember

- Inspire and motivate your team
- Guide your people's actions
- Anchor your brand promise and values
- Be meaningful to leadership, employees, potential hires, and customers
- Align with your aspirations and passions
- Define your reason for being
- Avoid jargon

This is why we emphasize the importance of identifying your purpose, then distilling it down to one word. The goal is for the one word to encapsulate your larger goal in a way that's easy to remember and live every day.

1. **Set aside a time to identify your mission—and put a limit on it!** Whether you are a team of one or many, it's important to set aside a sacred chunk of time with no interruptions: turn the smart phone and devices *off.* We recommend you leave your facility so you give your brain an opportunity to be stimulated in a new way. A new location = new ideas.

   Set aside no more than two hours. That's right, we said *no more.* Leaders can spend countless hours, even *days,* drafting, writing, and editing a long and onerous mission statement. In our approach, you have a deadline.

   When you walk out of the room, we want you to know your mission and be able to articulate it to others. A deadline will force you to be decisive, concise, and clear. At Kinesis planning sessions, we typically distill our client's mission in our planning sessions within forty-five minutes—even if they come into the room without ever having given it much thought. So two hours is more than adequate.

Whether you are a start-up or a company with a fifty-year old history, the process works in the same way. Regardless of your company's age, you can distill your reason for being into a One-Word Mission™.

2. **Forget tactics.** Once you are in the room where you will be brainstorming, acknowledge that this will be the anchor of your culture and your brand moving forward. That means you are looking to identify the beliefs and values you will use to guide more practical and tactic-based areas of focus for your company.

Avoid the temptation to get tactical in this session. For the linear-thinkers among you, rest assured that the checklists and goal setting will come. This session is about being an idealist.

Collins and Poras identified five important characteristics of a company's core purpose/mission:

- It's inspiring to those *inside* the company.
- It's something that is as valid one hundred years from now as it is today.
- It should help you think expansively about what you *could* do but aren't yet doing.
- It should help you decide what *not* to do.
- It's truly authentic to your company.

Defining your mission is all about clarity, authenticity, and alignment. This means that you do not have to sound "sexy." This is not something that needs to look impressive on a billboard. It does, however, have to feel significant to your team and your organization. After leading this process with many executives, we can say that when you finally identify your mission, you will feel a sense of conviction within you. You will sense a deep *yes* when it is uncovered.

3. **Identify your core purpose by asking the right questions.** First, start your session with the question: "How do we make the world a better place for our core customer?"

    Begin to write down all of the ways that you improve your customers' lives. And get very specific about the key differentiators that you provide—the solutions your business offers that make you exceptionally valuable and unique to your customers. (Don't worry about getting it down to a One-Word Mission™ yet—we'll get there. For now, you're just listing all the ways you provide value.)

    We realize that this will be easier for some types of companies than it will for others.

    At first, you will most likely write down things that are more practical then ideological. For example, "We build exceptional websites," and "Our professionals are experts in accounting," and "We help companies use the best technology to make better decisions."

    While true, these statements are not your reason for being. You need to go deeper. A powerful way to gain clarity about your company's purpose is to ask several rounds of whys.

    Start with the question "Why is this important?" Ask this same question repeatedly. After several rounds of whys, you'll find that you're getting down to the core purpose of your organization. You will start to articulate the very soul of your organization.

    Here are some additional *why* questions that can help you:

    -   Why is what we make/do important to the people we serve?
    -   Why does our organization's existence matter?

- Why do our employees dedicate their precious time, energy, and passion to our company?

Why is it so important to ask these kinds of questions?

Kinesis has a client that is a reseller of a specific type of enterprise software. When we first started working with them, they were stumped because they saw themselves as a commodity company.

However, as we talked more and worked through the questions above, we uncovered that their approach to servicing their clients was unique—their approach tied together various software solutions in a cohesive way that made their clients' companies more efficient and productive. They operated as consultants, partners, and complex problem-solvers, not simply software resellers.

Once they came to this realization, it became much easier to drill down to their core purpose. The way in which they serviced their clients was specific to their organization—and much different from their other competing resellers.

To be clear, your purpose does not have to be your strategic differentiator (although your differentiator can help you in your work to identify your mission). In fact, you can have the same or a similar reason for being as another company, even one that is in an entirely different industry.

For example, both an interior design company and a landscape company might have the purpose of "bringing beauty to people's lives." A puzzle company and a team-building event organization may both "provide tools of imagination." An analytics company and a private investigation business might both "solve the complex challenges that others can't." You get the idea.

Here are some examples of core purposes from Fortune 500 companies:

- Merck: To save and improve human life
- Walt Disney (original): To make people happy
- Mary Kay: Help women achieve personal growth and financial success
- Starbucks: To inspire and nurture the human spirit — one person, one cup, and one neighborhood at a time
- Amazon: To be Earth's most customer-centric company, where customers can find and discover anything they might want to buy online . . .

4. **Distill your core purpose into a One-Word Mission™.**

> "If the leader of the organization can't clearly articulate WHY the organization exists in terms beyond its products or services, then how does he expect the employees to know WHY to come to work?"
>
> —Simon Sinek, *Start with Why: How Great Leaders Inspire Everyone to Take Action*

Once you have defined your reason for being/core purpose, the next step is to distill it down into a One-Word Mission™. Yes, just one single word.

Kinesis developed this process with our clients in order to create a central theme that can be remembered by everyone in your company. One word is about as easy as it gets. And we've found this approach to be transformational in its ability to deliver meaning and purpose to the employees of an organization.

One bit of advice we give to companies is to think of their company as a schooner. These sailing ships possess a bottom-most structural element called a keel which runs along the centerline of the ship, from the bow to the stern. The keel is responsible for two primary functions:

- The keel gives a boat greater stability and control, preventing it from being blown sideways across the top of the water by the lateral force of the wind.

- The keel is made or filled with high-density material such as concrete or metal. This creates ballast or weight to hold the boat right-side up. Insufficiently ballasted boats tend to tip—or heel—excessively in high winds. Too much heel may result in a boat capsizing.

Essentially, the keel keeps the craft on the desired course and it keeps it stable. Think of your mission as the keel of your organization. It serves to provide your company with greater stability, control, and steadfastness.

Because of this, we recommend that your One-Word Mission™ be a noun. Nouns stabilize a sentence. They are the central building blocks of language. The rest of the sentence—verbs, adjectives, adverbs, and prepositions—revolve around the nouns.

If you haven't done so yet, take a look at the core purpose that you developed in the last section and work to distill it down to just one single noun. One technique for boiling your core purpose down to its essence is to fill in the blank of the following sentence:

"We are in the business of delivering X."

(X is your mission.)

At Kinesis, our reason for existing is to transform companies and brands, as well as the lives of the people who work there. We distilled this purpose into the One-Word Mission™ of Transformation. Everything we do is about transformation. We transform our client's companies, their cultures, and the way they serve their customers. We transform their brands, websites, and logos. And we positively transform the lives of the people who work for us as employees at Kinesis.

If at some point, we decided to offer a new service line, this is the compass that we would use to test it. For example, let's say we wanted to consider hosting websites as a way to expand our service offerings. Hosting websites is a commoditized service and is not particularly transformational. Because it's out of alignment with our mission, it would be a bad choice for our company.

During our planning session with the software reseller we mentioned in the previous section, their leadership team realized that their core purpose is to be a consistently reliable and dependable partner to their clients—a company that could always be counted on. They distilled this down to their One-Word Mission™:

Reliability.

Here are some examples of the One-Word Mission™ of some of our client companies. We've listed the type of service they provide and their One-Word Mission™.

- Wealth management firm: Intention
- Plumbing company: Empowerment
- Demand generation company: Results
- Precision CNC machine shop: Innovation
- Analytics management firm: Guidance
- Software development company: Simplicity
- Security and compliance provider: Dedication

5. **Talk about your mission with internal and external customers.**
   When you talk about your mission, you make it real. During your staff meetings, emphasize your mission and how it connects to the issues at hand. During new employee onboarding, describe your mission and how it will impact and shape the new hire's job and the goals they are working toward.

   And during your sales process, mention your mission—it will differentiate you and help you attract your right-fit customer who aligns with your mission. And you can certainly describe it in your marketing materials and website. Even though your mission is only one word, the more you give it cultural context by talking about it, the more power it accumulates.

   Below are several examples of how our client companies describe their missions:

   Commercial HVAC company: *Balance*
   Balance is the essence of our business. Balance is living in comfort; it's trusting in the systems that support you; and it's achieving sustainability in your life and in your work.

   Precision CNC machine shop: *Innovation*
   Our mission is innovation. We're reinventing precision machining. In everything we do—from customer service to the tools and technologies we use—we continually seek to find a better, more efficient way of manufacturing.

   Wealth management firm: *Intention*
   We take an intentional approach to helping you realize the full potential of your wealth. The very foundation of our company is based on our mission of "intention." It's the core purpose of our business, driving every decision and action,

and providing the foundation for how we approach our clients and our work.

Collections agency: *Betterment*

This means we are continuously striving to better our company, relationships, and processes. To do this, our team measures, monitors, analyzes, and improves productivity, systems, tasks, and ourselves to satisfy our clients.

So now it's your turn. Distill your core purpose into one single noun—your One-Word Mission™. You'll be amazed at the power of the One-Word Mission™. From there, write a sentence or two that provides context for your mission that you can share with your employees, prospects, customers, vendors, and referrers.

Remember, a deeply held mission will give your organization a strong sense of identity and continuity. It will give your team members a deeper understanding of your company's existence—one that goes beyond just making money. People fundamentally want to know that what they are doing serves a greater purpose.

A deeply held sense of purpose leads to excellence. Expressed as your mission, it serves as your company's keel, providing stability, control, and steadfastness.

Next, we'll look at the core drivers that shape your company's decisions and behaviors: your values.

PRINCIPLE #3

YOUR VALUES
MUST BE ALIVE

"It's not hard to make decisions when
you know what your values are."

—Roy Disney, co-founder of The Walt Disney Company

BEFORE YOU GO ANY FURTHER, TAKE A MOMENT AND WRITE down your organization's core values without looking them up. If you don't remember them verbatim, that's okay. Just get down their essence. (If you haven't developed them yet for your organization, that's okay too. We have a process to help you further along in this chapter.)

Next, write down at least one way your company values impact your daily responsibilities and activities.

Finally write three specific ways your values shape your company and/or team as a whole.

Was it hard to remember your values or was this exercise easy for you? What about how your company values impact your daily responsibilities? Or how values shape your team. . . . Did answers come quickly to mind, or did you find yourself scratching your head?

If you are like most of our clients, then you don't have your values memorized, although you might have been able to capture the essence of one or two of them. But even if you can list your values, you may have found that you came up short when it came to listing ways your values directly affect your day-to-day activities or your interactions with your team.

This is a problem. Values only work when they are implemented.

As a business professional, you've probably read lots of articles about the importance of values and values-driven companies. We certainly have.

Management books and business publications frequently espouse their importance. Best-selling business authors such as Jim Collins, Tom Peters, Simon Sinek, Patrick Lencioni, among many others, agree that having core values is essential to enduring business greatness.

And we agree. They ARE important. Crucially so.

When crafted thoughtfully and communicated effectively, shared company values can align employees and create a foundation for a passionate, committed, and engaged workforce, as well as greater revenue, increased customer satisfaction, and lower employee turnover—all of which contribute to greater profitability.

Unfortunately, while most companies have values that *sound* good, they typically consist of stale, meaningless jargon. No matter how poetic or lofty, hollow ideals will not only ring as inauthentic to your employees, they can actually impede your organizational performance. And, whether you store them in a digital folder or put them up on posters, unlived values have a way of fading into the background scenery. You'd probably be better off not having them at all.

Too many companies structure their values in a way that sabotages their effectiveness. And they lack a plan for putting their values into practice. Without the right structure and action plan in place to integrate values into a company's operations, values have no driving impact on a company's brand, revenue, sustainability, or differentiation in the marketplace.

Here's why.

Poorly structured, uncommunicated values fail to drive the decisions and behavior of your employees on a day-by-day basis. If your values are mere wall "eye candy" and leadership does not evangelize them, management will not know how to enforce them and no one in the company will live and breathe them. Even if leaders create their values with the best intentions, when these ideals exist only on paper, posters, and web pages, employees will perceive them as another out-of-touch management wish list.

Author Patrick Lencioni is even more pessimistic about the traditional approach to company values.

> I've spent the last ten years helping companies develop and refine their corporate values, and what I've seen isn't pretty. Most values statements are bland, toothless, or just plain dishonest. And far from being harmless, as some executives assume, they're often highly destructive. Empty values statements create cynical and dispirited employees, alienate customers, and undermine managerial credibility.[19]

After reading Lencioni's observations, it probably won't come across as a surprise that just 23 percent of U.S. employees strongly agree that they can apply their organization's values to their work every day, according to Gallup, and only 27 percent strongly agree that they "believe in" their organization's values.[20]

The most successful companies in Gallup's research, on the other hand, use values to shape their culture. And a great culture can be a formidable driver of company performance. These thriving companies in the Gallup research don't see culture as a stand-alone initiative; instead, they take a comprehensive and integrated approach to sustaining them.

Companies with strong cultures make reinforcing their values a constant priority. They take values from words to action and performance. They create messages around their values that communicate their desired culture to employees. And they create and implement programs that recognize employees whose work reflects their values.

"When it comes to organizational culture," write Gallup researchers Nate Dvorak and Bailey Nelson. "Values set the tone for how employees interact with others when representing the company. Values should be relevant to employees in everything from day-to-day tasks to company-wide meetings."[21]

We couldn't agree more. But one of the problems we see repeatedly is that the traditional approach to values fails, even when leaders try to operationalize them. Most values simply aren't written in a way that anyone can remember them, let alone act on them.

That's why we developed our method of identifying Living, Breathing Values™.

LIVING, BREATHING VALUES™ (LBVS)

AFTER WORKING WITH HUNDREDS OF BUSINESS LEADERS, we've created a precise formula to help you create Living, Breathing Values™ (LBVs) that are easy to implement and operationalize.

To be effective, LBVs must be remembered, understood, and used by your staff. They must work to inform each decision every member of your team makes, day in and day out. And—most important—LBVs must serve to inspire your people and help them understand how even the most mundane tasks are connected to the larger company mission.

By rolling out and operationalizing LBVs, leaders can make a very public statement about what matters most to your organization. These values will guide your employees on what actions they should—and shouldn't—take to uphold your brand at all times, even when their manager isn't present. And they tell your customers what your stand for as a company.

"Employees' behavior has direct impact on the bottom line, costs, revenue streams, level of productivity, customer satisfaction, even the brand—every aspect of the business is affected," writes business guru Tom Peters. "If strategy and culture are not aligned, the culture may support behaviors that conflict with what has to get done—and actually block execution of the strategy."[22]

To be effective, your values must be:

1. memorable
2. easily repeated
3. succinct
4. actionable
5. associated with your company beliefs
6. based on the leadership's passion
7. part of your daily culture
8. used to set employee goals
9. a measure of employees' performance
10. wrapped into your sales and marketing goals
11. connected to your mission and vision
12. integrated into the way you do business
13. aligned with your customer service delivery
14. linked to the way you differentiate your brand

And our methods for creating LBVs meet all fourteen of the criteria on this list. We know that's a tall order to meet and understand that, at this point, you may be a bit skeptical.

We don't blame you. Actually, we think you'd be crazy to not be at least a bit doubtful, especially given how many companies miss the mark when it comes to identifying and living values. There are too many platitudes posted on too many placards on too many walls. There are too many leaders paying too much lip service to values that do not inspire, engage, or motivate. There are too many articles on the power of values that never give actionable methodologies for effectively weaving them into your organization.

And—at the ugliest end of the spectrum—there are stories of scandals at companies like Enron, WorldCom, Lehman Brothers, and Wells Fargo that can sour even the heartiest optimist. These organizations no doubt had web pages or marketing materials touting their lofty values. Their *behavior,* on the other hand . . .

But despite all of the undelivered promises of leaders and organizations to be true to their stated values, we invite you to take a leap of faith and join us on this journey.

Because what we've seen again and again is nothing short of extraordinary. We have seen companies that have implemented LBVs transform into amazing cultures of A players who are fully engaged and who deliver exceptional customer service. Their employees report that not only do they feel more satisfied, but they think a great deal more about the future of their organizations.

What's more, our clients also have phenomenal outcomes from a revenue and profits perspective. Below are the results of three of our clients who are absolutely committed to living and breathing their values each and every day. Their CEOs, managers, and leaders make it a priority to weave their LBVs through every single facet of their organization. And they hold every single person in their company to that high standard of excellence:

- Client #1: Analytics consulting firm: In 2016, the company's revenue surpassed $4.4 million, a 958 percent increase from 2012.

- Client #2: Industrial energy consultancy: In 2016, the company's revenue was $17 million, a 386 percent increase over 2012.

- Client #3: Custom home construction company: In just two years, the company's revenue climbed to $42 million, a 1086 percent increase over where they had been when they started working with us.

While we can't guarantee you results quite as amazing as those of the rock stars above, we *can* promise you that the process of identifying and operationalizing your LBVs can have a profoundly transformative effect on your culture and your bottom line.

Let's dive into the methodology of crafting your Living, Breathing Values™.

VALUES AS VERBS

YOUR VALUES ARE NOT LOFTY INSPIRATIONS BUT RATHER a strategic decision-making tool for everyone from your CEO to your intern. In every moment, a person should be able to ask themselves "Am I in alignment with our values?"

Remember the schooner metaphor that we mentioned in the last chapter to describe your organization? If your One-Word Mission™ is the keel stabilizing your organization, then your LBVs are the winds that propel your sailing ship forward.

To be effective, your LBVs <u>must</u> be actionable—they are what will drive the behaviors within your company. This means that they have to start with a verb.

At Kinesis, our core values are "Think Big," "Build to Last," "Share the Good," and "Do the Right Thing."

So before they take any action, our employees ask themselves:

- Am I thinking big?
- Am I building to last?
- Am I sharing the good?
- Am I doing the right thing?

And if they answer no to any of these questions, then they are out of alignment with our values. They should stop whatever they are working on—whether it's a process, solution, presentation, answer, or action—or they should find a way to make a shift in the task at hand so that they can answer yes to all four of our LBVs. This is non-negotiable.

That means your leadership must also hold itself up to the same high standard. In every action you undertake, you must also be in absolute agreement with your LBVs.

It's time for you to write your Living, Breathing Values™. Here are the basic steps:

1. **Set up a time to meet with your leadership team.** When you get together, start by brainstorming a list of those qualities that you place a high value on. Often these are the same values that serve as standards for conducting your personal life. For example, you might come up with honesty, high-quality service, working as a team, creative problem solving, and so on.

Each person on your team can answer these questions to get the ideas flowing:

- What do I believe I personally bring to work each day?
- What does my work truly stand for?
- What does our company and brand stand for?
- What qualities do our customers believe about us?
- What behaviors should we expect from every employee (including me)?

Write all of the qualities on a whiteboard or flip chart so that the entire group can see these (if you are a leadership team of one, feel free to do this exercise on a piece of paper).

We also often ask the leadership team we are guiding to think of one or two ideal employees and write their names down on the board. Then ask: what does so-and-so embody that makes this person such an amazing fit for our company? What do these individuals value? This exercise will help you understand your values from a different perspective and bring additional ideas to your brainstorming session.

2. **Look for central themes.** Once you've reached agreement on the big concepts that reflect the qualities you value, your next step is to begin to lump together like qualities—think of it as a central theme for each group. For example, "dedication" and "commitment" are similar. So are "win-win relationships" and "build partnerships."

Once you have the core concepts lumped together, narrow it down to three or four groups. Do not have more than four—it becomes hard for people to remember. Your work is to come up with simple, broad values that will encapsulate your core beliefs.

This isn't easy, but it might help if you think about which concepts are absolutely essential to your workplace environment and truly represent the primary behaviors your organization wants to encourage in every person who works there. What concepts support your unique culture? (Note: If you currently have a culture that isn't what you want it to be, then you can make these aspirational. They can represent what you want to be as an organization.)

3. **Now start pairing the ideas with verbs.** All of your verbs should be action-oriented. Some popular verbs that our clients have used include: accelerate, advance, be, build, create, deliver, develop, do, elevate, empower, give, go, make, push, respect, support, think, and uphold.

    Keep each value short and sweet. The power of LBVs is in their simplicity. Each LBV should only be three or four words. To be effective, LBVs must be easy to remember and simple to say.

    Resist the temptation to develop additional LBVs. Yes, we realize that it is difficult. It is hard work to encapsulate your team's core beliefs into a few pithy phrases. But, we have worked with many company leaders who have been able to make this happen so we have faith in your ability to succeed at this task.

When we lead a session with our clients to develop their values, we have three simple rules:

• **Start with a verb:** LBVs are something you *do*. They are actionable, decision-making tools. As such, they must be a sentence that starts with a verb so that each person can ask themselves "Am I doing this?" and be able to easily answer yes or no.

- **Keep 'em short and sweet:** Limit each LBV to a few words. Most of our clients' values are four words or less. Some of our clients have articulated potent values with two-word sentences like "Own It" and "Think Big." Short and memorable = powerful.

- **No more than four:** Don't be scared of simplicity. Three is a great number and we even have a client with two LBVs that get the job done. We've found that people have a hard time remembering more than four values, so five is too many.

  You'll know when you're getting close to your LBVs because the energy level of the group will rise. People will be getting more excited about the best-fit ideas and words. When you nail it, you'll feel a resounding yes inside you.

  To help you out, here are some examples of LBVs that our clients have developed. You'll see that some companies have similar values while others have created unique LBVs. Since one of own values is "Share the Good," you are more than welcome to incorporate any of these LBVs into your own list:

  Industry: Residential Plumbing
  - Work as a Team
  - Elevate Your Game
  - Do the Right Thing
  - Own It

  Industry: Precision Machining
  - Push It Forward
  - Improve It
  - Go Further
  - Create Win-Wins

Industry: Collections Agency

- Respect People
- Exceed Expectations
- Be a Great Neighbor
- Maximize Client's Return on Investment (ROI)

Industry: Accounting

- Think Like an Owner
- Communicate Fluently
- Deliver on Your Promise
- Practice Awesomeness

Once you have refined your list of LBVs, we recommend that you and your leadership team "play" with them for the next week or two: charge every leader with putting them into action as they go through their day-to-day activities. Use them to make decisions—and only move forward with an action if it supports your LBVs. If it doesn't, make a change or say no to the choice.

Many of our clients find this to be an incredibly powerful exercise. As each leader interacts with staff, clients, and prospects and asks themselves if they are aligned with each LBVs, they often find that they must "up-level their game."

For instance, one executive at the software reseller we introduced in the last chapter reported an immediate and profound shift in his actions after his team identified "Build Sustainable Relationships" as an LBV.

During each interaction with another person, he asked himself, "Am I building a sustainable relationship right now?" He reported back that he tested this on the phone with prospects and customers, as well as during in-person conversations with his managers and programmers. With this question guiding his actions, he felt smarter and more thorough, and realized he was providing more value to people both inside his company and out.

For example, he told us about a specific conversation with one of their clients who was frustrated with an aspect of the software his company had helped to set up. As the executive spoke with his client, he kept thinking about building sustainable relationships and framed all of the solutions he suggested with that value in the forefront of his mind. In another scenario he described to us, he had a meeting with a couple of team members to talk about monthly sales quotas. The executive reported that framing the quota discussion with the value, "Build Sustainable Relationships," transformed their approach.

After your leadership team has lived your values for a week or two, reconvene and talk about your experiences. Ask each person on your team:

- How did you feel when you put the LBVs into action?
- How do you think this will help the company?
- How do you feel this will help your department?
- Does every LBV still feel right or do any of them need to be adjusted slightly?
- What can we do once we roll out our LBVs to help our team uphold them?
- Can we apply these in all situations with both external and internal customers?

If your beta test uncovered the need for any revisions, make them. Sometimes you simply need to add a word. Other times, you may find that the questions aren't helping you achieve the objectives you'd intended, so you may need to rewrite them.

Question six above (Can we apply these in all situations?) is a particularly important one. In addition to being an internal decision-making gauge for your team members, your LBVs also function as an outward-facing tool that your company can use to attract your dream clients (more about this in Chapter 5). When your marketing materials and your sales team incorporate your LBVs into the way you talk about your company, you'll attract clients that are an excellent fit.

The leadership team of one of our clients was particularly excited about their LBV "Enjoy Your Work." At first glance, this seems like a no-brainer. A culture of engaged employees should enjoy interacting with team members and bringing value to clients.

Unfortunately, as we drilled down a bit, we realized that not everything we do in business is enjoyable. For instance, handling a customer complaint gracefully is not always going to be fun. Nor is doing the hard work of cutting budgets or letting someone go. But, these are still things that must be done—and your LBVs should be a guide for the tough moments as well as the good times.

As we talked through this with our client, they decided to revise this one core value to "Help Each Other." This value is much stronger because it can be applied to internal and external customers in both positive, fun interactions as well as those scenarios that are quite difficult. We can always be helpful, add guidance, and support both our team and our customers—even if it's not a joyful situation.

ROLLING OUT YOUR ONE-WORD MISSION™ AND LIVING, BREATHING VALUES™

ONCE YOUR LEADERSHIP TEAM HAS FINALIZED YOUR ONE-Word Mission™ and LBVs, it's time to roll them out to your team (we recommend presenting them together). Whether you are a company of ten individuals or one hundred, this is a very important step in the process. Your people need to see that their leaders are passionate and committed to your new mission and values.

You can be as creative as you like with the process. We've had some clients who have started by introducing the managers to the One-Word Mission™ and LBVs first. After the managers familiarize themselves with the One-Word Mission™ and LBVs and begin to use them in their day-to-day operations, they take the mission and values company-wide. Some companies create events to recognize or reward those who are already living the values in their daily work.

Other clients have chosen a lower-key approach, such as sending out an email or printed newsletter from the CEO announcing the changes. This low-key roll-out was particularly effective for a security guard service—a company whose staff members worked at various physical locations and therefore didn't have many centralized meeting opportunities.

Later, the company used the One-Word Mission™ and LBVs in their regular leadership team meetings, recognizing employees who'd been living those values. For instance, some of their security officers were required by their certifications to pass a fitness test. The CEO awarded employees who improved their times and strength that year with the "Do It Better" award showcasing that these individuals were living that value.

Develop a plan for the launch of your One-Word Mission™ and LBVs that will engage and excite your management and your team. Think about what will work best for your company and people. Be sure to talk to your managers regularly to ensure they are using the One-Word Mission™ and LBVs on an ongoing basis with their direct reports.

ROLLING OUT YOUR ONE-WORD MISSION™
AND LBVS TO EXTERNAL CUSTOMERS

TO EFFECTIVELY APPLY YOUR ONE-WORD MISSION™ AND LBVs to your external customers, encourage your employees to weave your mission and values into conversations not only with prospects, but also vendors, customers, referrers, and business networks.

The CEO of one of our client companies—John Osser—runs a very successful company in the skilled trades industry. He told us about an innovative way of using his mission and LBVs that we hadn't considered. He was in the process of overhauling some of his partnerships with his professional service providers including his insurance company, attorneys, and accountants. After one and a half years of leveraging his LBVs to shape his external culture and relationships with customers, he realized that he could add a layer: by finding professional service providers and vendors that were in alignment with the company's core ideologies. So, he interviewed several companies in each category.

His interview consisted of a tour of his facility, which is an amazing example of a company in full alignment with its mission and values. After the tour, he would talk in depth about his mission and LBVs, explaining all the ways that his company was different and remarkable. He then asked potential partners about their own company values, mission, and what made them different.

His final selections were based on vendors' enthusiasm and commitment to their own companies' culture and remarkability, along with the philosophical alignment of the two companies' mission and values.

As a result of aligning everything with the company's LBVs—including his professional partners—John's company has realized incredible results. His profits are up significantly, the clients they work with are drawn to his values (and many of his newer clients are much bigger and more well known that before he began this work) with a 46 percent increase in new customer acquisition. Perhaps the most outstanding shift is that his employee retention rate has sky-rocketed. They lowered their employee turnover rate from almost 10 percent to near zero, according to John.

CREATING CULTURAL CONTEXT FOR LIVING, BREATHING VALUES™

AS A LEADER, IT'S YOUR JOB TO MAKE YOUR ONE-WORD Mission™ and Living, Breathing Values™ a core part of your company's culture. In other words, you should never stop talking about them and what they mean to your company, your employees, and your customers:

1. **When you post a job description, include your mission and values.** This helps filter out people who aren't the right fit for your culture and attract the ones who are.

2. **When you hire new employees, kick off their onboarding with a thirty-minute session with the CEO.** In this session, welcome them personally and tell them why the company mission and values are so important to you.

    We urge you not to defer this responsibility to a human resources director or manager. When the CEO takes time out of her or his busy schedule to impress the importance of the mission and values to the new hires, the passion can be contagious.

    At Kinesis, for example, Shawn spends time with each one of our new hires to introduce her or him to our mission, values, and vision. He tells them what they mean to him, as well as how we use them to inform our decision-making. This has a very powerful effect on each new hire, impressing the importance of our core tenets and the weight we place upon them.

At Rackspace (a website hosting company), they have a week-long orientation called "Rookie O." The sessions the new hires go through include the founders, C-level execs, vice presidents, directors, and others. The top-level folks share their histories and dreams and share what they find magical about Rackspace, including its culture and values.

3. **Bring the mission and values up at each and every staff meeting.** Get creative. For instance, one of the things we do at every one of our Kinesis monthly meetings is "Share the Good." At the end of our meetings, we ask each person to talk about something another team member did that was awesome. It reinforces this LBV and really makes people leave our meeting feeling good.

One of our clients—a medical eye clinic—has "call outs" at each staff meeting. Team members spend time recognizing when someone has exemplified an LBV by providing exceptional care to one of their patients. This reinforces both the importance of the LBVs and the right employee behaviors.

4. **Incorporate your One-Word Mission™ and LBVs into your performance reviews and goal-setting**. We encourage all our clients to set goals that are connected to their mission and values. And then, when it's time for your semi-annual or quarterly employee reviews, evaluate performance based on how well they met their goals—in other words, how well they lived your mission and values.

5. **Make sure managers reinforce your mission and values.** Regardless of their department, managers should praise people for living up to your mission and values. For example, one our clients, a manufacturing company, has the LBV "Make It Better." Their managers are able to tell a front-line technician who reorganizes an area on the shop floor or initiates some other improvement: "Hey, thanks for doing that. Way to make it better!"

Another client—a fabrication and manufacturing firm—brings their LBVs into all of their management meetings. The managers use this time for troubleshooting. For instance, Manager Raul Vargas might say, "Hey, since we've hit the rainy months, I have this situation in warehouse 2 where the employees are tracking in mud on their boots and no one is taking responsibility for mopping. What do you think I should do to get everyone to pitch in?"

During these problem-solving sessions, the CEO—Josh Steichler—provides advice to managers that is *always* framed by the values. To address the muddy boot issue, he might say something like "Until the issue is consistently resolved, hold fifteen-minute weekly huddles for the warehouse 2 employees and remind them about how important dry floors are to shop safety. Emphasize two of our values that apply: "Own It"—meaning they have the responsibility when they notice a hazard to clean it up (even if they didn't create it)—and "Win Together"—remind them that we are a team and when we all commit to making our work area safe, we all benefit from it. And then ask them if they have additional ideas that will help us live our values to help in this situation."

6. **Create a Kudos board.** This can be done in a variety of ways. One of our clients has a large board in the back area where their technicians come in to pick up supplies. Whenever a customer says something complimentary about a technician, it gets posted on their board so that all of the employees coming in and out can see it. Each testimony is paired with one of the company's values.

Another client has an intranet where the leadership can post great feedback from customers or managers. Because almost all of the employees in this particular company sit in one large call center, the CEO had a large electronic board set up on a high wall where everyone can see it. In addition to company updates, electronic recognition posts for the employees are showcased there as well. Again, all comments are paired with one of the organization's values to reinforce them.

Both of these companies exist in industries rife with high employee turnover and a dearth of great talent. Since establishing their One-Word Mission™ and LBVs and making them an integral part of the way they do business, their retention has improved tremendously. They now have almost zero turnover and attract a high-caliber of employee who is aligned with their values.

KEEPING THE VALUES ALIVE

FOR MANY LEADERS, KEEPING YOUR VALUES ALIVE AND breathing will be one of the most difficult part of the Marketing From the Inside Out® implementation. We call them Living, Breathing Values™ because they should be part of each and every decision your team makes.

We gave a few ideas about how to weave your mission and values into your culture, but it's up to you to be innovative and find many different ways to deliver the same information, over and over and over. Remember: you want to emphasize your One-Word Mission™ and LBVs on a daily basis.

We'll provide a word of caution here. In our experience, many leaders are hesitant to repeat themselves. They think that their employees will be bored, annoyed, or insulted. Or they believe it's a waste of their time. Redundancy feels wrong—it seems inefficient. Also, leaders themselves get bored with hearing their own messages repeatedly. Then, later on, they are surprised when team members don't know their mission or values.

In fact, internalizing your messaging is not an intellectual process—it's an emotional one.

That's why the big consumer brands have the same taglines, slogans, and messages year after year. Because they know that it fosters brand loyalty.

Think about your favorite songs. Why do you love them? Most likely, it's because you've heard them in a variety of settings and you have a fond association with these melodies. You may even be able to sing the words. Or think about college and professional sports teams. Fans who regularly attend their games enthusiastically participate in the same team chants over and over and over. This is the power of repetition.

Take advantage of this psychological phenomenon to create loyalty among your employees. One of your key jobs as a leader is to maintain your brand—and this requires a cohesive culture. So don't be afraid to talk about your One-Word Mission™ and LBVs over and over again.

YOUR VALUES HELP CUSTOMERS UNDERSTAND YOUR DIFFERENCE

MAKE SURE THAT YOU EXPRESS YOUR ONE-WORD MISSION™ and LBVs in your marketing materials and on your website. Help your sales team and customer service reps understand how to talk about your mission and values with prospects. Build a careers or culture section of your website and showcase stories of your employees living your mission and values. Write articles on your blog that tell stories of how your people are living examples of your mission and values. These actions will help you tell your unique story and set you apart in your industry.

Steve Jobs once said: "Marketing is about values. It's a complicated and noisy world, and we're not going to get a chance to get people to remember much about us. No company is. So we have to be really clear about what we want them to know about us."

Jobs says this so perfectly—the way you convey your mission and values to your employees and customers will ultimately ensure your long-term success as a company. The truth is, people become more emotionally connected to purpose-driven brands and the story behind them. And your ability to demonstrate the role your mission and values play in your story will drive loyalty and create memorability, leading to more word-of-mouth recommendations.

The human brain is wired to become more activated when it hears a story. Across centuries, around the globe, and in every culture, humans have told stories to share, remember, and understand the world around us. Stories can be told by a tribal elder explaining how zebras got their stripes, or by a parent perched on the side of their child's bed at night reading *Peter Pan*. They can be told on a Broadway stage to a large audience, or via a nighttime Netflix binge.

Regardless of the venue, our brains are hardwired to be story processors. Think about that as you roll out your One-Word Mission™ and LBVs to internal and external customers. How can they shape your brand story?

One of our clients helps companies produce their branded promotional materials. They have multiple locations with a number of employees who frequently travel to customer offices. To keep everyone connected to the mission and values, as well as each other, the CEO sends out a monthly newsletter. In it, she provides updates and inspiration, and much of it is framed by their mission and values.

Another client—a manufacturing firm—recently integrated their mission and values into a retirement party for a long-time, beloved employee. They guided everything from the invites to the talking points of the CEO's speech of recognition.

As you showcase your mission and LBVs in all of your marketing—both internal and external—people will more fully understand the importance your company places on its core tenets.

LIVING AND BREATHING YOUR VALUES TAKES FORTITUDE

COMING UP WITH AUTHENTIC VALUES THAT YOUR ENTIRE company lives and breathes—from CEO to intern—takes guts and commitment. Everyone in your company must not only embody them, but also enforce them.

This work will require reflection and discussion. It will also take maniacal commitment to enforce your mission and LBVs in all your systems—everything from hiring, orientation, and training to policies and procedures, performance and evaluations, and long-term business decisions. Leadership must take every step to ensure that your mission and LBVs are actual building blocks of your operations and culture, with intolerance for any violations of values. As you move forward, you'll minimize turnover by only hiring people who share your mission and core values.

When you first put your mission and values into place, you should know that the shift will be painful. Holding everyone in your organization up to the mirror of such high standards will cause some people to leave your company. You may have to fire some people. Even your best employees might give some push-back until they start to see the pay-off of using your values in their decision-making processes.

During the tough moments, simply remember that building an enduring business that stands the test of the time takes grit and determination. If this work were easy, everyone would do it.

But, in our experience, while building a great culture isn't easy, it is the most valuable thing that any company can do.

PRINCIPLE #4

YOUR VISION SETS
THE COURSE

"If you want to reach a goal, you must
'see the reaching' in your own mind before
you actually arrive at your goal."

—Zig Ziglar, motivational speaker and author

So, first of all, what is a Big Vision?

OUR DEFINITION IS PRETTY STRAIGHTFORWARD: A BIG VISION is a written description of what success looks like for your company at some point in the future. It should be both strategically sound and inspiring. It should motivate your people and set their course. Think of your Big Vision as a rallying cry for the people in your company to work together to achieve a dream.

Some other things a Big Vision can do for your company:

1. It clarifies your senior leadership's understanding and views about your organization's long-term direction.

2. It provides lower-level management with a tool to help guide their departments.

3. It reduces aimless decision-making at all levels of your company.

4. It provides your employees with an overarching purpose for their day-to-day tasks and conversations.

5. It helps your company set its strategic goals and objectives.

6. It assists you in preparing for the future (hiring, purchases, product/service decisions, etc.).

7. It provides a unifying force for your company by bringing employees together to work toward a single common goal.

In working with the leaders of many small- and mid-size businesses, we have found the Big Vision to be one of the hardest components of Marketing From the Inside Out®. While there are a few CEOs who immediately say to us: "Yes! I know exactly what where I want to take my company," these individuals are definitely the exception, not the rule. Most of the clients for whom we've helped identify their Big Vision find it an exciting—but very challenging—exercise.

Imagining the future state of your company isn't easy. So, as you begin diving into this chapter, if the visioning process feels tough to you, know that you are not alone. It may not be something that you can do right away—instead, it might take weeks or even months. In fact, it's better not to set your Big Vision too quickly or with too little thought. It should be approached with understanding and deliberation. And despite the effort it can take to work toward a bold

Big Vision, leaders who have done this work have found it to be well worth the time because it not only illuminates your path forward, but it allows you to set a series of planned, coordinated actions that will move you toward your desired, future state.

Take Ari Weinzweig, the cofounder of Zingerman's Delicatessen, who started his small business in Ann Arbor, Michigan, in 1982. Thirty years later, the company has grown into eight different businesses with seventeen managing partners, five hundred employees, and a revenue of $37 million a year.

"It's safe to say that we wouldn't be where we are without visioning," says Weinzberg. By getting people to start thinking about what success is going to look and feel like, creative, out-of-the-box ideas flow more freely. It gets people to go after the future of their choosing.

"When we do effective visioning," he says, "we're moving toward the future we want, not just reacting to a present-day reality we don't like. . . . Having a vision makes decisions much easier: The only opportunities even worth considering are those that are going to help us attain our vision."[23]

In a recent study, *State of the Business Owner (SOBO)*, representatives from the companies EMyth and PixelSpoke conducted research with more than seventeen hundred business owners from small- to mid-sized companies with an average gross annual revenue of $4.6 million and a median age of ten years.

One of the three key factors SOBO investigators identified was a written vision (the other two factors are plans and data). And yet only 42 percent of the businesses surveyed had a written visioning description of the desired future state of their business.

Amazingly the companies that *did* have a Big Vision grew 50 percent faster, were more optimistic about their future, and were 30 percent larger than those that did not. What's more, the owners of companies with written visions took home 25 percent more in compensation compared to the companies that did not.

If you conduct a Google search on writing a vision, you'll find a lot of different approaches. We like to keep the Big Vision simple. Why? Because, much like your One-Word Mission™ and LBVs, we want every one of your employees to be able to remember it. We want all the people on your leadership team to be able to bring it up with their direct reports. Your Big Vision is a dream that you can easily share with your prospects, potential talent, team, customers, vendors, and referrers.

Take a look at how some organizations articulate their Big Visions:

- Avon (beauty products): "To be the company that best understands and satisfies the product, service, and self-fulfillment needs of women—globally."
- Ducks Unlimited (preserves wetlands): "Wetlands sufficient to fill the skies with waterfowl today, tomorrow, and forever."
- Raytheon (provides defense systems): "To be the most admired defense and aerospace systems company through our world-class people, innovation, and technology."
- Haley Aldrich (consultants): "Be the company most sought after to integrate technology and human potential to tackle tough issues facing the world."
- Cork Supply (cork supplier): "Being the wine industry's most trusted and relied-upon partner."

RedBalloon is an Australian company that helps people gift others with experiences instead of products. It was founded by Naomi Simson in 2001 out of her house with a $25,000 personal investment. For every booking, RedBalloon takes a small commission.

Simson said people didn't understand her business at first. In the beginning, she recalls, she had to beg people to list with the company. "They, of course, didn't understand it, didn't understand the internet. It would take a lot of effort just to get a supplier." She would also take red balloons with their website URL emblazoned on them, tie them on her briefcase, and walk areas where big businesses were likely to see her. "Starting a business, you can't be proud." she said "You roll up your sleeves and you do whatever you can."[24]

It took more than two months for the company to make its first sale of a stress-busting massage. RedBalloon's profit? A $9 commission. Not exactly an earth-shaking beginning. But Simson kept working to get more and more suppliers to list with her company and, gradually, the list of experiences grew.

The company started gaining traction about six months after its founding. Fuji Xerox decided to purchase RedBalloon experiences as incentives for its sales team. With the multinational company's testimonial added to its website, other large companies including Qantas, Telstra, Westpac, and Commonwealth Bank followed suit.

By offering everything from sailing lessons to bungee jumping to a fashion makeover, RedBalloon stayed fully committed to its mission of *changing gifting in Australia forever.* And so, in 2005, as the company picked up steam, Simson and her leadership team decided to set a Big Vision of *providing 10 percent of Australia's twenty million citizens with a gifted experience.* Simson says, "It seemed like such a far-away dream (we had only done a few thousand experiences at the time)."

To keep the company's Big Vision visible to everyone, she installed a large LCD in the lobby that displays a running total of the number of experiences gifted to people. The screen is updated instantly when each experience is booked.

In her book, *Ready to Soar*, Naomi writes about the display:

"I love scoreboards—of every description," Naomi says. "I love numbers . . . I also like the scoreboard of where I sit against the rest of the population. And I can dial in to the RedBalloon scoreboard from my smart phone."

And on October 16, 2013, at 10:41 a.m., Simson announced on her company blog that they had achieved their Big Vision of two million customers. She wrote: "Today is a humbling day for me. It took ten years to ship the first million RedBalloon vouchers—and it took just more than two years to ship the second million. . . One experience at a time, day in day out, relentlessly we have focused on building our brand by how people talk about us."

As of 2016, the company has more than 3.5 million customers and is selling more than three hundred experiences each year.

That is the power of a Big Vision. The company understood where they were going, what the dream was, and how they would know when they had achieved it. It excited and energized the team (even though it seemed like a huge, crazy goal at the time).

"Many people are scared of the word *big*—what if you set out to do something massive and you don't get there?" Simson writes. "It will be okay! Often in business it is the same—because we don't know how to do something 'big,' we stop dreaming or creating. Write something that would be 'big' when it comes to your business idea. At this point, just have fun with it—write as many as you like; nothing is too outrageous."

Moz is another example of a successful company that had humble beginnings. In 2000, Rand Fishkin dropped out of the University of Washington to work at his mother's small business marketing firm as a web designer. In 2004, he created SEOmoz blog, which over the next decade became the world's most popular online resource for search marketers. In 2007, he became CEO of Moz, the company he cofounded with his mother based on his blog's success. As CEO, he grew the company from $800 thousand to $29.3 million.

Moz's Big Vision helps focus their strategy and initiatives to accomplish goals. It kept the company from getting off course. Their current Big Vision, which was set in June 2013, is "One million people paying to use Moz's products by May 29, 2018."

"Once you have the vision for your company set," Fishkin says, "so many things that were hard (what projects to say yes/no to, who to hire, how much to invest, whether to raise money or go solo, what to prioritize on your road map, how to rate your performance, etc.) become so much easier."

A BIG VISION KEEPS YOU FOCUSED

REMEMBER THAT SCHOONER SHIP METAPHOR WE USED IN the last two chapters? If your mission is the keel that keeps your organization stable and upright, and your values are the driving winds that move you forward, then think of the vision as the destination that you've chosen—it's the port across the ocean that your team is steering you toward.

Without a vision, your organization is adrift. Sure, you'll eventually end up somewhere, but will you—as a leader—be happy with the result? Without a Big Vision in place, your destination is a crap shoot. Do you really want your future to be left up to chance? Or would you like it to be intentional?

A clear Big Vision will help guide strategy, align decisions, and bring purpose, motivation, and focus to your employees. It is, quite simply, a picture of what success will be at a particular point in the future. It answers the questions:

- What does our company look like X years down the line?
- How big are we?
- What are we known for?
- How do people feel about working here?
- What have we accomplished?
- How do we know we've arrived?

And at first glance, vision-setting sounds like a simple concept. After all, we all dream about the future, keep "bucket lists," and imagine ourselves achieving great things in our lives.

And yet, we've watched many of our clients struggle with this task. Often their visions are overly complicated and difficult to remember. Worse they just don't get them excited (and if the leadership team isn't excited, you can bet your employees won't care either).

Let's look at another famous Big Vision—one that captivated the world—and one of the most impressive when we take into account how impossible it seemed when it was shared.

In 1961, John F. Kennedy stated his vision to the world. It was big, bold, and awe-inspiring. "I believe that this nation should commit itself to achieving the goal, before this decade is out, of landing a man on the moon and returning him safely to earth," he said. "No single space project . . . will be more exciting, or more impressive to mankind, or more important . . . and none will be so difficult or expensive to accomplish."

While Kennedy had received assurances that such a voyage was possible, the technology necessary did not yet exist. In other words, JFK had no idea *how* NASA would ever achieve this vision.

Why set such an audacious goal?

According to the NASA historical archives, JFK was motivated by a number of political factors: First, he felt a great deal of pressure to have the United States "catch up and overtake" the Soviet

Union in the space race. In 1961, the nation was shocked when Soviet cosmonaut Yuri Gagarin became the first man to orbit the earth. In addition, the Bay of Pigs botched invasion earlier that year had put enormous pressure on the Kennedy administration. He needed to do something big to restore America's confidence in the United States' capabilities as well as his own leadership.

Kennedy asked Vice President Lyndon Johnson to poll leaders in NASA, industry, and the military. Johnson reported that "with a strong effort" the United States "could conceivably" beat the Soviets in sending a man around the moon or landing a man on the moon. Kennedy also had assurances from NASA's Deputy Administrator Hugh L. Dryden who wrote that there was "a chance for the United States to be the first to land a man on the moon and return him to earth if a determined national effort is made." However, Dryden also told him that the earliest this feat could be accomplished was 1967, and that to do so would cost about $33 billion dollars (a figure $10 billion more than the whole projected NASA budget for the next ten years[25]).

Despite the fact that in 1961 there was no rocket powerful enough to send humans to the moon and back, computers were not up to task, and no one knew how to keep a person alive in space, JFK's Big Vision sparked action and it motivated people to reach further.

Thousands of the nation's engineers, scientists, researchers, designers, programmers, and politicians began to work furiously. And they were met along the way with various challenges and setbacks including the tragic loss in 1967 of three astronauts who died in a fire during launchpad tests at the Kennedy Space Center in Florida.

Despite the hurdles, in just eight years, the United States was the first to land a man on the moon. What seemed impossible when JFK shared his Big Vision became a reality in July of 1969.

While your vision might not take you as far as the moon, you can harness this same power of inspiration in your company.

HOW DO YOU SET YOUR COMPANY'S BIG VISION?

A GREAT BIG VISION STRETCHES THE IMAGINATION. IT'S A far-reaching point on a map that sets your direction. From there, you can create a detailed strategic plan that tells you how to get you there.

Some important things to keep in mind while setting a Big Vision:

- A Big Vision does not have to be about growth (although it can be).
- You don't have to know HOW you will accomplish your Big Vision.
- You Big Vision is specific enough that everyone will know if you've achieved it.
- Your Big Vision will take years to accomplish—we recommend looking forward at least ten to twenty years into the future (although in certain quickly moving industries, it might be better to only look five to ten years out as the Moz case study demonstrated above).
- Keep your Big Vision short and clear.
- Think BIG—It should be passionate, aspirational, and ambitious. It's your Mount Everest.

Setting Your Big Vision

1. **Once again, get out of your office!** If you are the CEO and are going to set a Big Vision on your own, then go to your favorite

quiet spot—the beach, mountains, or quiet room. Then turn off all of your media. This means no smart phone, tablet, laptop, Bluetooth device, or desktop computer.

If you are working as a leadership team, then go to a quiet room with a whiteboard—one that's outside of your building. Get plenty of healthy food to eat, lots of coffee and water, and turn off your devices.

2. **Ask yourself where you are now and where you want to go.** Start by reviewing your One-Word Mission™ and LBVs. Why do you exist? What are your Living, Breathing Values™? Who do you serve and how do you provide value to them?

Ask yourself what you specifically want to achieve: what problem does your company exist to solve? Who is your target customer base, and what do you want to do for them? This information will help you get grounded in the now—so you can begin to get more clarity about where you dream of going.

Lean into the future and imagine where your company will be in ten to twenty years. Fantasize. Wonder. Be curious about what's possible. Ask questions like:

- What is happening in the future?
- What does success look like?
- When you overhear people talking about your company, what do they say? What's the buzz?
- What are you best known for?
- What have you achieved?
- How are you changing the world for your customers?
- What are you accomplishing?
- What remarkable milestones have you achieved?

- Imagine your company is being described in a top industry publication ten to twenty years from now. What do they say about you?

You can brainstorm a number of components to your Big Vision—get as creative as you'd like. Don't be afraid to be unconventional. Be sure to write everything down as you come up with ideas. Many of these ideas might be useful tools to incorporate in your company as you move forward.

Remember to dream big and don't worry about the *how*. Focus on your success. Right now, this is all about creating an imaginary future—the *how* will come later. This should be a fun exercise in which you can go all out in really stretching your imagination. It's a journey of discovery.

3. **Distill your ideas into a single sentence.** Go back and review the examples of Big Visions we shared earlier in the chapter. Notice how each company staked a big, bold claim? Their visions both inspire and evoke emotion.

While we encouraged you to put a time limit on the process of identifying your One-Word Mission™, it may take you several days or weeks to condense all of your ideas around your vision into a concise sentence. Why? Because your Big Vision will shape everything your company does moving forward. The work you invest to get to this one key sentence will provide valuable clarity about who you are as a company, who you will be, and who you don't want to be.

Brevity begins with long drafts. So don't be scared to start with a paragraph (or even a page). But then, ruthlessly edit that paragraph again and again and again until you have a sentence—or two at the most—that your employees can memorize, repeat, and move toward. Ultimately your Big Vision will inspire and guide your organization's efforts both now and in the future.

4. **Communicate your Big Vision.** After deciding on your Big Vision, the most effective way to get your company moving in the same direction is for your leadership team to develop a clear message about what you decided, and then communicate this to your direct reports. Then tell those people to go and share the message with their direct reports. In using this cascading communication approach, it's important to make sure the messaging is consistent and occurs quickly after you finalize your Big Vision. Help each team member to understand how the Big Vision relates to their day-to-day responsibilities.

    Once your Big Vision is communicated throughout the organization, your leaders and managers should begin to have conversations with their teams. Invite feedback and ask for examples of how everyone's work is contributing to the Big Vision. Encourage their recommendations for improvement.

    Your company's leaders cannot be aloof. They must get in the middle of the action and communicate what success looks like. This is what will inspire their teams to follow suit.

5. **Make your Big Vision part of your brand story.** Your Big Vision should be a story you tell again and again and again. Bring up the Big Vision at staff and management meetings, use it in your conversations with potential new hires, tell your salespeople to share it with your prospects, and use it in your goal-setting and performance-review meetings with employees.

    Dennis Crowley, CEO of Foursquare, says, "One of the lessons we keep learning over and over again is the value of repeating the vision and talking to as many people as you can—over-communicating actually—just so we all know why we are doing this and why it's important."

As a leader, one of your most important jobs is to clearly and passionately communicate your company's Big Vision, underscoring its relevance. Bold ideas communicated effectively are what inspire people to do more than they thought possible. Through your words, actions, communications, events, and meetings, talk about the future and share the vision—doing so is a powerful way to drive employee engagement. The more you share it, the more your Big Vision will gain momentum within your organization, helping to motivate them to "reach for the moon."

KNOWING YOUR DREAM CLIENT IS CRUCIAL TO GROWTH

"Know what your customers want most and what your company does best. Focus on where those two meet."

—Kevin Stirtz, speaker and author

Do not skip this chapter.

YOU MAY START READING IT AND SAY TO YOURSELF: "OH, this chapter is about my target audience. That's Marketing 101." And it's true, identifying your core customer should be one of the foundational components of your marketing strategy.

That said, it's also one of the things that most small- to medium-sized businesses get *wrong.* Virtually every client we work with starts with one or more of the following problems:

1. **They're targeting too broad an audience:** What we often hear is something like "Oh, well our audience is everyone." Or "We serve everyone in the X industry." But we find that a lot of companies are marketing by casting a wide net, when what they really need is a targeted spear gun.

2. **They've identified the wrong buyer:** This happens when marketing and sales is targeting a person/position in the potential client company who isn't the true decision-maker.

3. **They don't know where to look for their target audience:** There are ways to find your target audience—certain events they're likely to attend or a media they typically use. But many companies don't have a strategy for seeking their customers where they're likely to find them.

4. **They have not accurately defined their target customer:** In our process, we recommend clients take a deep dive into thinking about the target audience—developing a thorough profile so they know exactly how to attract their DREAM clients.

So we challenge you—what do you really know about your core customer? And, taking it further, do you know all of the qualities your dream clients possess? We're talking about the ones who bring you the most profit, are easy and fun to work with, respect your expertise, stay loyal to your company, and refer new prospects like crazy!

Your ultimate goal is to get to a place where every single customer in your company is a dream. We'll show you how.

1. **Start with the basics.** Hopefully you are already well acquainted with your dream client's demographics—things like:

- Age
- Generational cchort
- Location
- Gender
- Education level
- Social class
- Marital status
- Family size
- Life cycle stage
- Income
- Occupation
- Job title
- Industry
- Ethnicity
- Size of company
- Annual revenue of company
- Type of company
- Industry

(Before you get started on this list, read on for a bit because we're going to ask you to list a number of characteristics to help you develop a complete persona profile.)

2. **Get personal.** The next piece of the puzzle is your dream client's psychographics—the more personal characteristics of the people you are targeting. Think about:
   - Personality traits
   - Beliefs
   - Attitudes
   - Values
   - Personal interests

- Leisure activities
- Hobbies
- Lifestyle
- Behaviors
- What do they wear?
- What do they drive?

3. **Think about the best qualities of the clients you already have.** Now think about all of your current clients. (We understand this isn't possible in all instances, especially if you have a large customer base. That's okay, just pick your top ones).

    Of your current customers, who do you like working with the best? Which clients value your offerings the most? Write down both the company and the first name of the person in the company who you work with the most. You may have one crème de la crème client. Or you may have several. Either is fine. This is to help you build lists of the characteristics you most appreciate in your clients.

    Once you have your name(s), go back to your demographics and psychographics list. Do these clients fit what you wrote? If not, you may need to rework your original descriptors to match the names you listed.

    If you have multiple distinct offerings, you may have multiple dream clients. Just repeat this exercise for each grouping. Some of our clients develop a matrix because they have very distinct targets that they market to in different ways.

    What makes your dream client?

4. **Identify your dream clients' characteristics.** Your next step is to write down all of the factors that make each name on your list a dream client. This goes beyond demographics and

psychographics. Here's what some of our clients have come up with:

- Aligns with our values and mission
- Excited about our Big Vision
- Pays on time
- Profitable
- Refers new work to us
- Fun
- Friendly
- Respectful
- Asks us to do more work for their company
- Loyal
- Tech-savvy
- Intelligent
- Motivated
- Team player
- Values our work
- Is a champion for our company
- Doesn't nickel and dime us
- Is in one of our growth industries
- Isn't a PITA (pain in the ass)
- And so on . . .

5. **Create a persona for each of your dream clients.** Since each of your clients may only have some of these qualities, feel free to create a composite dream client. You can choose a real or a fake one. In this exercise, go as far as you can to develop an intimate profile. Imagine sitting next to them having coffee. Now ask yourself:

- What drives them at work?
- Who is their boss?

- What makes them look really good in their position?
- How crucial is the purchase of your service to their role? (In some types of purchases, making the wrong decision could cost a person their job.)
- How does your offering fit into their company goals?
- What is this person looking for in a service partner?
- What is keeping them up at night?
- What are their true pain points? What causes them to feel frustrated, overwhelmed, upset, exhausted, and so on.
- Is this person the true decision-maker? Or does someone else hold the purse strings?
- How long are they typically in this position in their company (is it a position that turns over frequently, or do people stay in it for decades)?
- If this person were your prospect, what would make them sign a contract today?
- What could derail the deal?
- Do they sit at a desk all day? Or are they traveling most of the time? Or are they on a factory floor?
- Are they in an industry that is innovative or lagging?
- What keeps your customer loyal to your company?
- What makes their job hard?
- What do they value?
- What are their career aspirations?
- How will they find your company? (i.e. search engine, trade show, work of mouth, etc.).
- Who is influencing them—both internally and externally?
- What information sources do they trust?
- What type of content do they prefer? And how do they consume it?
- What information do they need from you?

- How are buying decisions made in their company?
- What is their typical day like?

By answering all of these questions, you can develop a buyer persona for each of your dream clients. Creating these mini-biographies will help you better empathize with your clients and understand their user experience and how they make purchasing decisions.

Your goal is to create a detailed sheet describing each dream client that you can share with salespeople or anyone else in your organization who plays a role in sales or marketing.

If you have a hard time developing the profile or answering the questions listed above, then interview five to ten of your best customers and ask them how they would answer these questions.

6. **Identify your dream clients' pain points.** You are in business because you provide solutions to your customers. You've got the expertise and the answers to a specific set of problems.

That doesn't mean you understand your buyers' true motivation for buying—or that you understand how to market and sell to them.

Your first inclination may be to approach the situation logically by presenting rational data, facts, and systems. After all, emotions and business don't mix, right?

Wrong. Emotion is the strongest driver of choice, loyalty, and advocacy. No matter what you sell or who you target, never forget that your buyers are people and people inherently make emotional decisions.

While consumers might think their decision-making is based on reason, it's actually heavily influenced by subconscious emotional factors beyond their awareness. Harvard

Business School professor Gerald Zaltman says that 95 percent of our purchase decision-making takes place in the subconscious mind.

"There is a lot of research across disciplines showing that human beings aren't as logical as we'd like to think," said Anjali Lai, analyst at Forrester Research, Cambridge, Massachusetts. "We see ourselves as rational decision-makers, but that's only because we're not even conscious of how emotion is driving our behavior."[26]

"Results from Forrester's Customer Experience Index show that emotion is often the primary factor influencing customer loyalty," she says. "Emotion is often the strongest driver of customer retention, enrichment, and advocacy."[27]

So this is essential to keep in mind: buying isn't a logical process—it's based on a person's feelings. Your prospects' emotions come first, and then they use logic to substantiate their buying decision. So yes—especially with large purchases—your buyers will need facts, figures, charts, stats, testimonials, and so on. But they also rely on their "gut" to guide their purchasing behaviors.

Your prospect is feeling pain or fear around an issue—they have a gap, deficiency, impediment, and/or risk. In fact, unless your prospect has pains, they simply won't purchase your service or product. Their pain is what will trigger an emotional response, creating a sense of urgency and pushing them to make a purchasing decision.

According to Kevin Hogan, the author of *The Science of Influence,* "most people react to the fear of loss and the threat of pain in a much more profound way than they do for gain."

So what is causing your dream client pain?

Here are some business-to-business (B2B) examples:

- We don't have enough experience in our organization to solve this problem.
- This issue is taking too much time away from my primary responsibilities.
- I'm worried that our organization won't meet the requirements of a specific regulation or certification.
- The price of our current provider keeps increasing.
- Our current provider is not responsive/savvy/advanced enough.
- I'm frustrated by the inefficiencies in our organization.
- I want our organization to have an increased competitive advantage.
- We are facing a communication barrier.
- We are losing money with our current product/service and need to make a change.
- Our company is falling behind technically and we need a state-of-the-art solution.
- Our customers are expecting something different from what we have and we need to make a change.
- This year's aggressive growth goals won't be met unless we make a change.

Of course, this is just a short list—your dream clients may have entirely different sets of pain points. The following questions may help you uncover them:

- Why does my buyer need my offering?
- What frustrates my buyer in his/her job—and how might my offering help?
- What does my buyer not like about my competitors?
- What is causing my buyer to waste time, spend money, lose profits, etc.?

MARKETING TO YOUR DREAM CLIENTS

ONCE YOU HAVE IDENTIFIED YOUR DREAM CLIENTS AND their pain points, now you have the power to create targeted marketing and sales collateral. Your ultimate goal is to have these individuals look at your materials and think to themselves: "Wow! It sounds like they are speaking right to me."

Unfortunately, most companies—especially those in the B2B space—are seller-centric rather than buyer-centric. Their sales and marketing messages focus on all of the features of their offerings. But what your customers really want to know is: How can your solution fix their problem? And the more you can speak to them directly about their issues, the more likely you are to convert them into a buyer.

Now that you have a deep understanding of your dream clients, it's time to rewrite your marketing materials so that they truly target them.

More specifically, you can use this knowledge to write website, blog, video, email, and white paper copy that helps answer your prospects' burning questions and solves their specific problems. This type of targeted content can be used for both outbound and inbound marketing—when you write it specifically to your dream clients, you will reach more qualified leads while realizing a higher conversion to right-fit customers. Your new customers will be more loyal, profitable, engaged, and appreciative. And your team will enjoy working with them more. What follows are some strategies we have found to be particularly helpful:

1. **Describe your dream clients publicly.** Don't be afraid to define your target clients in your marketing materials. The Kinesis website gets pretty specific when describing our dream customer:

Kinesis works with a broad array of B2B companies, ranging from big data analytics to building science consulting. However, all Kinesis clients are service-centric—and share a few things in common:

- They have gross sales from $2 million to $30 million.
- They have a long sales cycle with low volumes and high margins.
- They have a unique approach that uses client education to accelerate sales.

In addition, we provide maximum value by working with people who align with our values and mission of transformation. The owners and leaders of our client companies:

- Are forward-thinking and strategic.
- Hunger for new insights and approaches to business.
- Want to grow a sustainable business with a strong, well-known brand.
- Are interested in positioning their company as a leader in their field.
- Care deeply about customer experience.
- Want a vibrant internal culture that runs smoothly and attracts the top talent.
- Seek a consistent marketing execution rhythm.
- Understand that marketing operates most effectively when it integrates with business strategy, company culture, and sales outreach.

This approach been remarkably successful in attracting amazing clients. Don't be afraid of specificity—paradoxically, even people and companies who fall a bit outside of your dream client descriptions (but still have most of the characteristics) will not be put off. Instead, they will be drawn to work with you.

One of our clients had a brilliant idea to help them attract their best-fit client. They developed a PDF that they could forward to their network or hand to people they know or just met. Typically, they share the document with people they have relationships with, and ask them to refer it to potential clients.

Let's face it, we are bombarded with so much information that, despite our best intentions, we forget a lot of things people tell us. So if we rely on verbal recommendations only, we risk our referrers forgetting what we said to them about our best type of client. This PDF jogs their memory, helping them to identify and refer the right people.

Another approach is to showcase the testimonials and success stories of your current dream clients. The cliché "like begets like" holds very true when it comes to attracting potential clients. As author Robert Cialdini writes: "Social creatures that they are, human beings rely heavily on the people around them for cues on how to think, feel, and act. Testimonials from satisfied customers work best when the satisfied customer and the prospective customer share similar circumstances. Influence is often best exerted horizontally rather than vertically."[28]

Showcase your dream clients and tell their stories in order to attract more just like them. Photographs and videos (on your website) make the narrative even more compelling.

2. **Define your core benefits.** Let potential clients know about the core benefits that your services and products provide to them. When working with clients, we divide the core benefits into three areas: functional, emotional, and economical.

Where many companies go wrong is by focusing instead on describing the features of their businesses and offerings—things like length of time in business, depth of experience, certifications, professional affiliations, technology, equipment, price, and mundane descriptions of services.

While these are important qualifiers for your prospects, they do little to nothing to differentiate your company from your competitors. Think of them like "table stakes"—the *minimum entry requirement for a market or business arrangement.* But your real competitive advantage goes a step beyond table stakes. Once your prospects have ticked off the industry-standard checkboxes, what else do you supply? What sets you apart?

We will make one disclaimer here—in some companies, certain features matter. For example, we have a high-end machine shop client that has purchased specific equipment and completed a multi-year ISO 9001 certification process. ISO 9001 specifies requirements for a quality management system where an organization demonstrates its ability to consistently provide products that meet customer and applicable statutory and regulatory requirements. Passing this certification sets our client apart from a large chunk of other machine shops. And so, they list these features, but they don't stop there—they also make it a point to emphasize additional core benefits. More about this in a moment.

Beyond the features your company provides, there are so many additional things that you can say in your marketing to highlight your remarkability. This is where knowing your core benefits comes in.

3. Know your core benefits

Functional benefits

As we mentioned, the first type of benefits is functional—in other words, the way in which you provide your services and products. Functional benefits include your processes and your method of doing things. For example:

- The internal memory of a smart phone
- The screen resolution of a computer monitor
- A toothpaste's ability to keep away cavities
- A convenience store that is open twenty-four hours
- The automatic updates of a cloud-based software
- Monthly reporting from an accounting firm

Functional benefits may be table stakes in your industry, or they may be unique and remarkable if you use a cutting-edge technology or have a new type of equipment. Such benefits can be a door opener for a while, but if it's a great idea, your competition will be able to eventually copy it. So market your exceptional functional benefits while you can, but don't rest on your laurels.

Emotional benefits

You may not have thought a lot about the emotional benefits of your offerings—and yet, emotions are what drive the majority of people's purchases. That's why it is so crucial to understand your dream clients' pain points, and the emotional benefits that you provide.

Your marketing may be rooted in the tangible, functional benefits, but the emotional, intangible benefits are what will motivate your prospects to convert and stay loyal. In addition, the brands that connect with their customers on an emotional level can charge a premium. Big consumer brands tend to be masterful at capturing the emotional benefits of their products:

Harley-Davidson: Harley has achieved brand excellence through emphasizing the emotional benefits of freewheeling self-expression. In a highly competitive marketplace pummeled for years by aggressive Japanese imports like Honda and Yamaha, Harley has held its own by creating and emphasizing an entire lifestyle around its motorcycles. They use emotional phrases such as "I love the freedom" and "How do you measure the value of the world opening up to you?" and "The meek inherit nothing."

As a result, Harley-Davidson has developed a fierce brand loyalty that most companies can only dream of achieving. Harley customers don't just ride the bike—they wear the T-shirt and the hat. They even get the Harley logo tattooed on their bodies. They feel as if they belong to a large family of Harley riders.

Apple: Apple have built a community of fiercely loyal customers by recognizing the pain of a clunky user experience. So, their products—Macs, iPhones, and iPods—are all sleek, elegant, intuitive and, above all, fun to use.

Apple recognizes that their customers embrace being different—they are a bit rebellious and reject the status quo (i.e., Microsoft and IBM). Steve Jobs appealed to his dream customer by declaring "Apple is about people who think outside the box, who want to use computers to help them change the world."

The company has touted the slogan Think Different and included iconic twentieth century personalities who went against the grain including Albert Einstein, Richard Branson, Amelia

Earhart, and Jane Goodall in their marketing. They have a unique verbal and visual vocabulary to reinforce their customers' emotional connection to the Apple brand.

Consider the following Apple ad, kicking off their Think Different campaign:

Here's to the crazy ones. The misfits. The rebels. The troublemakers. The round pegs in the square holes. The ones who see things differently. They're not fond of rules. And they have no respect for the status quo. You can quote them, disagree with them, glorify or vilify them. About the only thing you can't do is ignore them. Because they change things. They push the human race forward. And while some may see them as the crazy ones, we see genius. Because the people who are crazy enough to think they can change the world are the ones who do.

Ask yourself:

- What are the emotional benefits we offer to our customers?
- How can we leverage alleviating their pain points to create a customer experience that goes above and beyond that of all our competitors?
- How can we create customer service processes that accentuate our brand and create fierce customer loyalty?

Economic benefits

Some companies and offerings will have more economic benefits than others. But almost every service has at least a couple. We ask our clients to call these out as a distinct category because they can be very compelling motivators to a company's buyers. Economic benefits:

- Save you money
- Make you money
- Save you something that costs money (for example, a fuel-efficient car or an energy-saving stove)
- Save you time
- Reduce waste
- Increase productivity
- Improve sales/conversion rates
- Preserve revenue
- Avoid fraud
- Retain clients
- Provide opportunity for more business
- Increase profits
- Decrease overhead
- Increase capacity

One item that is technically an economic benefit that we recommend steering clear of is "we provide the cheapest option." This position often leads you quickly down the road to low profits, high churn, and commoditization of your products and services. Few small businesses have the outside capital and economies of scale to make this strategy work (in other words, unless you're Amazon's Jeff Bezos, look for other advantages).

4. **Working with clients in different industries.** If you work with several industries (some of our clients call these "vertical markets" or "verticals"), then separating out the industries into discrete categories on your website is a great strategy. On each separate page, describe the specific core benefits that you offer to each industry along with the expertise that you have that enables your company to be the best choice for your prospect.

You can also weave in testimonials and link to case studies from other industry-specific clients. This will help you down the road when you create marketing material for your various audiences. Your buyers want to see that you have specific expertise and attention in their industry.

Even if you are expanding into a new arena, include a page or section on your website describing that industry—you won't have specific examples, but some new clients might give you a try because they are impressed with your other qualifications if you can demonstrate how you will translate your expertise to their industry.

For example, we have a client in the manufacturing industry who really wanted to expand into aerospace and defense. They spent three years getting their facility up to speed (with equipment, systems, and staff training) and obtaining specific certifications that help to set them apart from competitors. The company clearly defined their new target client and their pain points, and explained they could provide them with the best solution.

In their marketing materials, they showcased their new certifications and demonstrated to prospects how their innovative machining systems and processes could help save money, reduce waste, and consolidate efforts in the prospects' manufacturing and logistics chain. They also used many custom photographs on their website to demonstrate the cleanliness, orderliness, and capacity of their facility.

In addition, we helped them overhaul all of their marketing materials to be in better alignment with their new prospects' expectations. The result was several multi-year, multi-million dollar contracts from some huge names in the aerospace and defense industries.

5. **Just say no.** Make sure to provide a detailed description of your dream clients to your sales team. And—here's the tricky part—be sure to also train them to say no to the people who are not a good fit. In other words, you do not want them to bring in new customers who are not your DREAM.

   Make it a practice to avoid working with any more individuals and companies that are what we call "PITA" (pain in the ass) clients. These customers take too much of your organization's time and effort. What's more, they are rarely profitable.

   You likely have PITA clients already. In fact, we bet you can think of at least two or three right now. Think low profits, low volume, costly to serve, late to pay, disrespectful, aggravating, demanding, etc.

   Know their names? We thought so. You do not want any more of them. Tell your sales team to think of your business as an exclusive nightclub: only a select few should get past that velvet rope. Yes, your company is that special!

   Be very clear with your sales team—not simply about your right-fit customers but also about who to turn away. Your sales team are the best people to hold that velvet rope, preventing the PITA clients into your company.

   "Most underperforming sales teams don't know who wants to buy their wares," says Dan Waldschmidt, sales trainer and author of *Edgy Conversations*. "They have not spent enough time researching their 'ideal target customer' so they try to sell to everyone. And that means that they don't have a high close rate, enough revenue at the end of the quarter, or enough morale internally to turn in outrageous sales results."

   "Fixing that is easy," he says. "Spend time saying no to the wrong prospects. And carve off time each month to refine your target customer model. Make it collaborative. Reward great ideas. Fight for clarity."

It's crucial to help your sales team understand exactly who makes a great customer, and who does not. Only half of the twelve hundred firms surveyed in a sales performance study report having an agreed-upon formal definition of what their company considers to be a qualified lead. Not surprisingly, the study also finds that of those with an agreed-upon definition tend to enjoy a significantly higher lead conversion rate.[29]

Over time, as your sales team begins to better understand the ideal, dream customers you want to bring on board, they will shift their selling methodology. Instead of trying to pitch someone who isn't the right fit for your company, they will begin to focus all of their efforts on locating new prospects who are aligned with your culture and excited about your offerings. These right-fit leads then convert into ideal customers.

Help your team by sharing a brief synopsis of what this prospect is like (industry, goals, pains, key identifiers, and what your company can do to help this person).

But don't stop there—communicate consistently with your sales team. Measure their performance against how effectively they set up meetings and close these deals.

And what's more, you can charge a premium for providing exactly what your dream clients desire—instead of trying to be all things to all people and competing as a commoditized business, you can be the premiere provider of the exact services your dream clients want.

This alignment is incredibly important. A client is an enormous asset to your business and they are also a major investment of your team, time, energy, and resources. And most of the time, this relationship results in significant benefits for both parties. You'll spend many, many hours getting to know the client's processes, politics, industry, goals, and marketplace.

In contrast, when a client is a poor fit and the relationship is a struggle, most (or all) of that initial investment is wasted. You typically spend hours of unbillable time putting out fires and feeling frustrated. When the relationship finally comes to an end, you often do not get the great referrals and "follow-on work." Even worse, the poor fits result in huge opportunity costs and a client with a limited customer lifetime value. It's also just not that enjoyable for any of your team.

But when your sales team learns to say no to the wrong-fit prospects and yes to the right ones, you will increase your revenue, profitability, and employee and customer satisfaction.

5-STAR CLIENT EXERCISE

IF YOU ASK ANYONE IN YOUR COMPANY TO IDENTIFY YOUR "best" customers, they may be able to rattle off a couple of names. Most likely, the list will include the businesses that are keeping your team very busy. However, this type of gut check is not in any way indicative of whether your client base is in alignment with your target customers—nor does it tell you anything about their profitability and cost to serve.

Yet many companies don't even attempt to take a basic look at which customers bring the most value to their businesses. They may group customers by market type or identify top accounts based on top-line revenue—but we urge companies to go further. Whether you have an inferior process or no process at all, you're missing an opportunity: Customers do not bring the same value to a business, so why do we treat them the same?

Let's answer that question by gaining more clarity about your current portfolio of clients with something we call the "5-Star Client" exercise. Basically, you will review your current customers and rank them based on the characteristics you listed above when defining the characteristics of your dream clients.

Start by listing your customers for the past year or two (feel free to go back further if you like—just make sure not to overwhelm yourself with data) in the left-hand column of an Excel doc.

Next, stratify them into three sections in your spreadsheet:

- Your dream clients—or those who come close: these should go in the rows at the top
- Solid or average clients who may or may not be exactly what you're looking for, but they're not a problem: put these in the middle rows
- PITA clients—these go at the bottom, under the other clients

Once you have your clients all listed, divide your spreadsheet into thirds. The group in the rows that make up your first third are your A-level customers, the middle third are your B-level customers, and the bottom third are your C-level customers.

Then—in the next columns—begin to list discriminating factors such as the amount they've spent with your company, their size, the type of work they have requested from your company, cost to serve, quality of relationship, and so on. This will help you further arrange your customers within each group: A, B, or C. The easiest place to start is total annual revenue spend and profitability. Even charting out just this information is a valuable start—you can always work in additional factors later.

Rank	Client	Revenue	Profit
A	Acme Co.	$10K	15%
A	Wayne Enterprises	$10K	10%
B	XYZ Co.	$2K	30%
B	Virtucon	$20K	6%
C	Tyrell Corp.	$3K	2%
C	Globex	$2K	-3%

THE SUPERSTAR CLIENT EXERCISE

THE NEXT EXERCISE IS FOR THOSE READERS WHO WANT TO go deeper (either now or down the road). It gets a lot more complex and requires you to collect significantly more data. However, if you weave in these elements, your ability to make decisions about your customers will be much more powerful. So, even if you aren't prepared to add these into your matrix now, review these items so you can begin to collect the metrics that will allow you to incorporate them down the road.

The right-hand columns in a spreadsheet will look different for every business. That said, here are some ideas to get you thinking:

- **Financial return:** Revenue, profitability, buying power, future revenue potential, volume, risk (for contingent projects in particular), cost to serve, etc.

- **Cultural alignment:** Does the client align with your values and mission? Do they value the expertise you bring to the table? Do they have a similar culture? Do you like them?

- **Relationship dynamics:** Do you have access to the right stakeholders? How difficult is it to create consensus/make decisions? Are they respectful? Do they meet deadlines? Do they value your services and team? Are they loyal?

- **Market dynamics:** Based on what you know or can project about fluctuations in the marketplace, is this type of work representative of a growing industry and therefore opportunity? Or is a contracting sector that will lose volume over time?

- **Strategic categories:** Is this type of work an area you want to expand into (for example, a new deliverable, new industry, new client type, etc.)? Does it align with the direction of your company vision?

- **Quality of work:** Do you and your team find this project/client work compelling and interesting? Is this the type of work that gets you excited? Will it keep your people engaged and motivated? Is this the type of work that will help to attract the best job candidates to your company?

- **Size factors:** Are there important factors that make a client an ideal fit for you based on size of their annual revenue, number of employees, number of physical locations, size of facilities, size of output, and so on?

Whether you choose to do the simple 5-Star Client exercise or the Superstar Client exercise, the stratification of A-, B-, and C-level clients will still be roughly in thirds.

One thing that we recommend—regardless of the level of complexity you choose—is to immediately move any customers that are not strategic for you into the C category *even* if they are profitable and have brought you good revenue in the past. A customer who isn't strategic is one that is not an ideal fit for any reason—they do not align with your mission and values, are in the wrong industry, are disrespectful and painful to work with, are not growing, and so on.

Now that you have your list together, let's briefly discuss the Pareto principle (named after Italian economist Vilfredo Pareto). It states that roughly 80 percent of the effects come from 20 percent of the causes. This means that your company has easy access to dramatic improvements by focusing on the most effective areas of your company and eliminating the rest. In the case of your now-stratified list of clients, we can use Pareto's principle (the 80/20 rule) to predict the following:

- 80 percent of your profits come from the top 20 percent of your clients.
- 80 percent of your revenue comes from the top 20 percent of your clients.
- 80 percent of your complaints, inefficiencies, and problems come from the bottom 20 percent of your clients.

Armed with this information, let's consider the top two-thirds of your A-level clients. This is the segment of your customers that should be getting the most attention. They are your best, cream-of-the-crop, VIPs, special-sauce clients. Give them love and nurturing so that you can grow these accounts even larger. We'll talk more about this in Chapters 8 and 9 when we discussion customer retention and account growth.

Now let's look at the middle level of your strata. Your bottom one-third A-level and top B-level clients are interesting. When you look at these, ask yourself "Why aren't these companies in the top

Rank	Client	Revenue	Profit	Strategic Fit
A	Acme Co.	$10K	15%	High
A	XYZ Co.	$10K	10%	High
B	Virtucon	$2K	30%	Low
B	Tyrell Corp.	$20K	6%	High

20 percent of our A-level clients?" In some cases, it may simply be because they are newer clients and haven't been a customer long enough to bring them into the revenue/profit levels of a top A. With these instances, just keep working on their longevity and they will move up into the A tier.

With other B-level clients, however, there may be other reasons why they aren't in the A tier. Some may not be as good of a fit as a dream client. But others might be missing some key information or service from you. And these are the ones that necessitate a closer examination. As you review these customers, ask your team:

- Does this client know about the entire depth and breadth of our services?
- Are we servicing them to the fullest of our capabilities?
- Is this client meeting regularly with an account rep?
- Are there additional problems this customer is having that we don't know about?
- Have we added as much value as possible to this customer?

Chances are that some of your B-level clients could be more fully served by your organization. With more information and a higher level of service from your company, some of these B-tier customers may just be A-level clients waiting in the wings for more attention from you. And, nurturing your B-level clients who already know, like, and trust you is much less expensive compared to new customer acquisition.

Next, take a close look at your C-level clients—especially the ones at the bottom. You'll typically find that these clients are bringing in only about 20 percent of your company's revenue and may not be very profitable. What's more, they take too much of your team's energy without a lot of reward. They are overly demanding and may not always pay on time. With these clients, it's time to "fire" them. With the ones who are too small for you but not a PITA, you can simply refer them to another business that could better take care of their needs (and be happy to have the account).

We know it can be painful to let go of clients who have brought you revenue. However, we've found if you continue working with clients who aren't the right fit, they will ultimately distract from your company's overall well-being. Not only are they not bringing your company enough profits, but they are a huge opportunity cost. Your team is spending too much time and energy taking care of their account when they could be focused on nurturing your A-level clients and expanding those accounts.

Empower yourself and your whole team to "cherry-pick" your customers and only work with the ones who are a true strategic fit, as well as those who are profitable, respectful, and loyal. In our experience, companies that seek out, sell to, and nurture their dream clients soon notice increased employee engagement, word-of-mouth referrals—and, of course, revenue.

PRINCIPLE #6

ONLY CASTLES WITH A HIGH, THICK WALL WILL LAST

"Differentiation is one of the most important
strategic and tactical activities in which
companies must constantly engage."

—Theodore Levitt, author and
Harvard Business School professor

IN JANUARY 2007, STEVE JOBS ANNOUNCED THAT APPLE
would be releasing a revolutionary new product: a cellular device
that would deliver all the features of an iPod.

Apple set up the release with a brilliant marketing campaign
that included a commercial which aired during the 2007 Academy
Awards. The iPhone was a dramatic departure from phones with
dials and buttons and this commercial visually conveyed the contrast. The commercial began with a black and white close-up of a
rotary phone from Alfred Hitchcock's movie, *Dial M for Murder*, followed by a quick montage of thirty-one different film and TV clips

with well-known Hollywood actors answering ringing phones with just a "Hello?"

The phones they are answering loosely march us forward in time until the spot finishes with a quick shot of the iPhone, followed by two black screens—one read "Hello" and, the other, "Coming in June." The ad ended with a white Apple logo against a black screen. For many, it was their first look at the iPhone and the "Hello" ad generated interest and intrigue.

When the technology was rolled out, it didn't disappoint. The 3.5-inch screen and touch-sensitive keyboard made the iPhone one of the most innovative products we've seen hit the marketplace in recent decades. By the fall of 2008, Apple became the most profitable phone maker in history.

The iPhone was a game-changer. Of course, the thing about changing the game is that, pretty quickly, the other players will make their way to your court. Just two years later, all the top-tier smartphones had traded in the sliding QWERTY keyboard that Blackberry had made popular for touchscreen technology.

Our point?

If a pioneering product with technology as complex as the iPhone can be replicated, then you bet your product and services can also be easily copied. And with the increasing amount of data available, the pace at which new technologies and innovative offerings become commodified will only accelerate. Anything you create can and will be replicated by your competitors in the blink of an eye.

But that doesn't mean you should feel paranoid or stop innovating. In fact, you should feel excited about the opportunities that competitive pressure can create for your company. With engaged employees and a forward-thinking culture, you can still create a competitive advantage.

Castles, moats, and curtain walls

Renowned investor Warren Buffet has been shaping global stock-investment viewpoints for decades. When describing the companies he looks to invest in, he said, "I look for economic castles protected by unbreachable moats."

In other words, Buffet highly values the competitive advantages that protect a company—its moat. He knows that only those "castles" with deep, wide moats will stand the test of time. A few examples of castles and their moats? Buffet likes Coca-Cola for having the strongest of economic moats—they are recognized as the world's strongest brand and have more than thirty-five hundred products available in nearly every country worldwide and they are able to charge 20 to 30 percent more than generic brands because consumers love Coke products and continuously purchase their favorite drinks. Buffet also describes the auto insurance company, GEICO, as having a deep moat of low cost. He says: "I mean people have to buy auto insurance, so everybody's going to have one auto insurance policy per car basically, or per driver. And . . . I can't sell them twenty . . . but they have to buy one. What are they going to buy it on? They're going to buy it based on service and cost. Most people will assume the service is fairly identical among companies, or close enough, so they're going to do it on cost, so I gotta be the low-cost producer. That's my moat. To the extent my costs get further lower than the other guy, I've thrown a couple of sharks into the moat."[30]

Now, that is certainly a sound investment strategy—but it's not really practical for small- and mid-sized business owners to emulate the competitive advantages of the Fortune 100 and Fortune 500 companies that Buffet is judging to make his stock portfolio perform better. So how can you apply this philosophy to your own business?

Enter the curtain wall.

We have borrowed Buffet's wide moat methodology and applied its basic principles to the act of protecting small- and mid-sized businesses from marketplace competition. We call this a "curtain wall" philosophy.

During the millennium that lasted roughly from the fall of the Western Roman Empire to the Renaissance, the development of medieval fortification made it almost impossible to get into medieval cities. During this period, considerable stone and other valuable resources, construction effort, and engineering skills were put into construction of curtain walls.

These thick outer curtain walls surrounded the whole of the castle complex. They had projecting towers to house soldiers defending the castle. They had battlements and walkways to support defenders and allow them to see and fire upon attackers. Many curtain walls were more than thirty feet high and they ranged from six to twenty feet in thickness!

Investors look to companies with an economic moat to make sure that it is maintaining a competitive advantage. Similarly, as a company leader you need to be thinking about how your company is fortified. We believe that you must build an impressive curtain wall—and it can't just be one that looks good—it has to be strong enough to provide a differentiation for your company, as well as keep out the competition and guard your talent.

How do you build a curtain wall?

Think of your curtain wall as the unique way in which your company provides products or services to both its internal and external customers. It's the combined elements of your company's signature approach that differentiate your brand—everything from your employees, culture, values, and processes to your customer service, tools, and leadership structure. Weave them all together and you have a competitive advantage that can't be copied.

Google is a good example of a company that has a formidable curtain wall. The organization is known for their extremely selective hiring process—they intimately understand exactly the type of person who will fit their culture.

But they don't stop there: they have team members who are dedicated to keeping their colleagues happy and productive. Once hired, Google employees get perks such as free meals, swimming pools, nap pods, video games, and more. This focus on culture has paid off, as Google consistently ranks among the best places to work and enjoys high retention in an industry notorious for talent-poaching. The company also has a proprietary approach to maintaining its search algorithms and is continuously evolving its products and infrastructure.

Clearly, they have the competitive advantage. As of October 2017, Google accounted for 80.6 percent of search engine traffic across the worldwide web, with competitors Bing and Yahoo!—both providing nearly identical services—trailing far behind with 7.51 percent and 4.51 percent respective market shares. While its unparalleled success is an obvious draw, Google's unique hiring and onboarding processes also continue to attract the best and the brightest.

Google understands that talent, culture, and innovative, unique approaches are crucial building elements to a curtain wall.

A curtain wall makes it harder for the barbarians (your competition) to steal your customers and talent—and it keeps your customers and employees warm and cozy inside your castle. They have no need or desire to leave.

So, what can *your* company do to fortify its curtain wall? What structural elements will really set you far apart from the competition? What processes and features will keep your customers from ever wanting to leave your castle?

Of course, you've already begun building your curtain wall by focusing on the innermost fundamentals of your fortress that we've already discussed in previous chapters—your mission, values, vision, and culture.

But there are three additional layers to your curtain wall structure which we'll cover in this chapter:

- Your Remarkable Selling Point: This is your company's competitive difference that is remarkable in your marketplace.
- Your Service Delivery Map: This is your unique, signature process that you provide to your clients. It describes the overarching, systematized method that you use to deliver your services.
- Productized signature services: These are services that you have packaged to make them repeatable, unique, and easier for your clients to buy.

When you adopt this three-pronged approach, you will realize multiple benefits:

- **You shape the brand experience for your customers** by creating consistent, signature processes that everyone in your organization can repeat. Think of a restaurant franchise. When you go into a McDonald's or Starbucks or Applebee's, it doesn't matter whether you're in Honolulu or Tulsa, you are going to have the same experience. No matter the size of your company or your industry, your goal should be to systematize your processes and experiences so customers know what to expect no matter who in your company they're interacting with.

- **You can train your new hires to live your brand.** When you develop repeatable signature services, you can ensure your newer hires deliver the same high-quality offering as your more experienced employees.

- **You can scale your business for growth.** Many service-centric businesses that we've worked with customize their services for every single client. But all too often, this results in them charging too low a rate because of poor estimates. When you standardize your approach, you decrease the time it takes your team to complete the project and simplify the delivery process. This results in higher profits and repeatable methods that are easier to scale.

- **It adds a level of professionalism and credibility** to your business. When you can begin telling prospects, customers, and potential talent that "we do things in this way" and follow that up with a detailed description of your signature method, you position yourself as an expert in your industry.

- **You widen the gap between your company and competitors.** When you take the time to create a Service Delivery Map and package your signature services, none of your competitors will be able to deliver services in exactly the way you do. The more you distinguish your unique offerings, the stronger your curtain wall will be.

- **It creates a longer revenue cycle with a client.** Many service-based B2B companies have projects or even project phases with very specific start and end dates that span a few months or quarters. Then, when it's over, it's time to sell that same client a new project or project phase. By developing a proprietary process for delivering your services, you can often extend the period of time in which you are doing business because you are selling a package that ties together multiple project phases.

Here is what the "selling one phase of project at a time" model looks like:

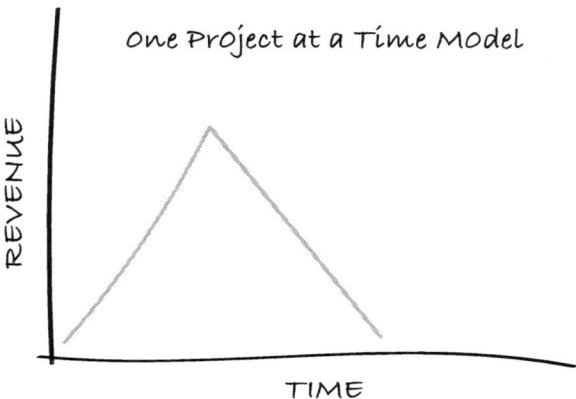

A single project provides a limited injection of cash into your business. Compare that to the signature method model we recommend which involves selling your phases as a package:

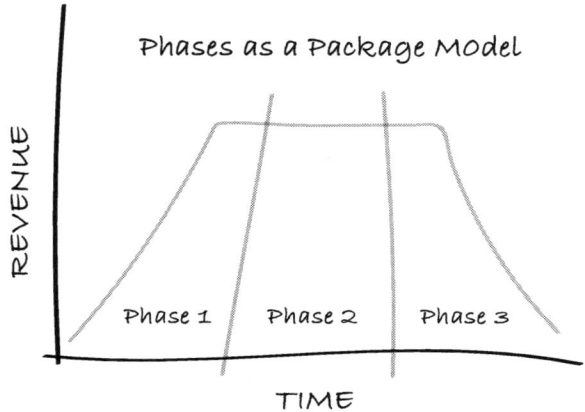

A package infuses more revenue into your business over time.

- **It accelerates sales conversions.** It is as easy (or as difficult, depending on your perspective) to sell a $100,000 project package as it is an $10,000 project. And sometimes it's even easier because bigger deals put you in touch with the real decision-makers from the get-go. Executives often want to purchase a multi-phase solution, unlike middle managers who may simply be looking to address a single pain point.

CURTAIN WALL PRINCIPLE #1:
IDENTIFY YOUR REMARKABLE SELLING POINT (RSP)

THE LEADERSHIP TEAM AT THE COMMERCIAL HVAC COMPANY WarmCool was facing a challenge that threatened the viability of the company—and their industry. For the last few years, ManpowerGroup's *Talent Shortage Survey* has reported that the hardest segment of the workforce to fill is the skilled trades—a skills gap that is only expected to grow. Of the 42,300 employers surveyed in 2016, more than 40 percent are experiencing difficulty filling roles. This is the highest level since 2007.[31]

At the same time, high school technical programs are being cut, vocational schools are closing their doors, and a high percentage of the skilled trades workforce is getting ready to retire. Unsurprisingly, the WarmCool team struggles to find capable mid-level and high-level technicians.

"Our historic methods for bringing in new people weren't working anymore," said the WarmCool president. "Since we couldn't find them, we decided to do something radically different. Now we grow them ourselves!"

Rather than relying on deteriorating recruitment and training methods for recent trade school grads, they decided to hire them right from high school—and develop a unique proprietary approach to train them that no other companies were doing.

WarmCool spent a year developing and documenting a comprehensive internal multi-year training program for new hires. They also partner each new hire with a mentor, an experienced senior technician who shows them the best ways to tackle real-world HVAC issues, as well as how to work with customers and deliver their service in the very specific way the company has developed.

What WarmCool did was essentially rewrite the book on growing the best workforce of tomorrow—instead of trying to compete with all the other companies using the same old methods, they built something remarkable. Their company has a formidable curtain wall.

In this section, we're going to discuss how to create your own remarkable company—and then figure out exactly how to talk about what sets you apart using a concept we call a Remarkable Selling Point (RSP).

You may be familiar with the terms "unique selling proposition" (USP) or "value proposition" (VP)—in other words, your unique position in the marketplace. Your USP or VP is a focal point that sets you apart from the competition and creates offerings that are particularly appealing to your dream customers.

We start there—but our approach is all about highlighting your remarkability.

In his book *Purple Cow*, author Seth Godin defines "remarkability" as something worth talking about. Worth noticing. Exceptional. New. Interesting. It's a Purple Cow. Boring stuff is invisible. It's a brown cow.

Most of your competitors will never do what it takes to create a remarkable company. Why? Because most companies will stop when things are simply *good enough.* Don't be like them. Go further.

Your goal is to avoid the trap of trying to please everyone and instead tell your dream customer exactly why they should purchase your remarkable products and services. An RSP is a clear statement of the concrete results your ideal customers will get from purchasing and using your products and/or services.

Your goal is to distill all the complexity of the value you provide into an easy-to-remember phrase that your client can grasp. Keep in mind that your RSP should identify an unmet need that your customers face—and offer a remedy. It should relieve their pain.

To start to uncover your RSP, ask yourself: Why should our dream customer purchase from our company and no one else?

Remarkable companies build things worth noticing into their culture, offerings, customer service, systems, hiring methodology, internal training, and processes. Like WarmCool, they are problem solvers, innovators, and industry leaders.

It may feel risky to be remarkable, but it's far riskier to stick to the status quo.

Consider what happened to the Blockbuster empire when Netflix showed up. Blockbuster was a very "fat" business that thrived from its neighborhood rental stores that offered newer releases. At its height, it had more than fifty million members worldwide.

When Netflix first offered its DVD-by-mail service in the summer of 1997, there were no real competitors.

A lot of people forget that the first Netflix model didn't work that well. It was clunky and logistically challenging. They were using the same model as Blockbuster—a set fee for each video rented. When Blockbuster set up its own mail-delivery service, Netflix's stock tumbled. In fact, Netflix CEO Reed Hastings approached then-CEO of Blockbuster John Antioco to try and sell the company he founded for $50 million.

Barry McCarthy, Netflix's former chief financial officer, said in an interview with the Unofficial Stanford blog in 2008, "I remembered getting on a plane, I think sometime in 2000, with Reed [Hastings] and [Netflix cofounder] Marc Randolph and flying down to Dallas, Texas, and meeting with John Antioco. Reed had the chutzpah to propose to them that we run their brand online and that they run [our] brand in the stores and they just about laughed us out of their office. At least initially, they thought we were a very small niche business."[32]

But here's where the story gets interesting.

Blockbuster was increasingly alienating its customers with its strict late fees and its stores' boring, warehouse-style spaces. And even though there were indications that video customers wanted something different, Blockbuster executives ignored the signs. They hired a new CEO who started changing their game plan, including pulling out of their internet efforts.

Around this same time, Netflix decided to make a radical change in the way people rented DVDs. Instead of fee-per-DVD, customers were allowed to pay a flat monthly fee and rent as many movies as they wanted with no late fees. They also got their delivery systems dialed in through establishing regional distribution centers. Netflix moved on to develop the technology that allowed them to stream internet movies to their customers—a video on-demand system whose algorithms helped people select movies based on their preferences. Innovation helped Netflix become the successful multi-billion-dollar company it is today, while Blockbuster declared bankruptcy.

Here's another one of our favorite examples of a remarkable company, FedEx. From its inception in the early '70s, the company took a very systematic approach to innovation.[33] Its original selling point was "When it absolutely, positively has to be there overnight." To deliver on their promise of overnight deliveries—something unheard of at the time—FedEx needed to be remarkable.

When the company began, the process of sending packages was largely a manual process. FedEx founder Fred Smith decided the status quo wasn't good enough. The company pioneered and developed technologies later embraced by many other industries such as an automated customer service center, a hub-and-spoke delivery system using both places and trucks, and overnight package delivery.

They also developed the tracking number—incredibly new at the time and now a standard in all shipping. In fact, Smith is famous for saying, "The information *about* the package is as important as the package itself."

The FedEx legacy of remarkability continues today. In addition to its long-standing commitment to technology and innovation, FedEx values its employees. It puts its people first and has been honored as one of the *Fortune* "100 Best Companies to Work For" ten years and counting. It is heavily committed to community service and environmental initiatives.

A more recent example of an innovative, forward-thinking company is Spanx. Founded by Sara Blakely, this company started with a core product that did not yet exist in the marketplace: slimming footless pantyhose. Blakely did not like the way her bottom looked in white pants and her feet got hot in her pantyhose. So she created her own version of what she imagined other women would want too.[34] With $5,000 of her own money, she produced and aggressively promoted the first prototypes. She could tell customers why they needed her product in thirty seconds using her RSP: "I've invented footless pantyhose so you can wear white pants with no panty lines, look thinner, and wear any style shoe."

She also realized the impact of showing people what was so remarkable about the product instead of simply telling them about it. Doing something creative and unconventional, Blakely took pictures of her own rear end with Spanx and without them. She would stand at the entrance of stores and if her quick explanation of her RSP didn't reel customers in, she would hold up her photos and they would say, "Oh, I see . . . I'll take two!"

That's remarkability in action. Because of Sara Blakely's willingness to take a risk and create something remarkable, people started talking about the amazing new product. Today Spanx does more than $400 million in global retail sales annually, with more than two hundred products carried by top retailers around the world.

Your RSP is the gateway into your differentiation. It doesn't have to sound sexy since it's not an outward-facing tagline, but it should be a concept that shapes your brand. Think of it as the secret ingredient that keeps you from being a "me too" company in your industry. If we looked at some famous companies and their RSPs, they might look something like this:

- **Zappos.com**—Almost any shoe you want with bend-over-backwards customer service.
- **McKinsey & Company**—You can hire the best minds in management consulting.
- **Google**—Provide access to the world's information in one click.
- **Southwest Airlines**—Low fares, lots of flights, lots of fun.
- **Rackspace**—Fanatical support. We're doing what it takes to make a difference for every customer.

Remarkable companies are ones that employees, customers, and referrers absolutely adore. Every day, they focus on creating services and processes that cater to their dream customers. They don't worry about attracting prospects who aren't a great fit. What follows are some thoughts about coming up with your own RSP.

1. **Be the best at something no one else is doing.** This may come as a surprise, but your RSP is not about being the *best* in your industry. Instead, it's about being the *best at something else no one is doing.* That's the approach Voodoo Doughnuts in Portland, Oregon, took when they opened shop. Most people would agree that they don't serve gourmet donuts. Given that you often have to wait more than an hour to get your doughnuts, they don't provide the quickest service. And they certainly aren't known for being the best restaurant in town.

   But they do completely embrace their hometown city's slogan: "Keep Portland Weird." As a result, you can count on Voodoo Doughnuts to sell you the most unusual doughnuts. You can get doughnuts covered with cereal, bubble gum, Oreos, bacon, or lemonade dust. You can also get one shaped like a Voodoo doll or—ahem—genitals. They are also open twenty-four hours so that you can pop in after going to parties and bars. And, of course, all of their confections are served in their hallmark pink boxes—their promise is that "good things come in pink boxes."

   "When Kenneth 'Cat Daddy' Podgson and I opened [Voodoo] we just didn't want to work for 'the Man.' We had been friends for about fifteen years and wanted to go into business together," says Voodoo cofounder Richard "Tres" Shannon. "We had the epiphany that there wasn't a donut shop in downtown Portland. There were plenty of donuts in town, but we couldn't find anything in the downtown core.

   "We put kind of funny toppings on them from the beginning—cereal and things like that. But the bacon [took a little while]. We used to put NyQuil and Pepto Bismol on our doughnuts in the first couple of months, but the FDA shut us down after a front-page 'Living Section' article in the *Oregonian* that said 'Night of the NyQuil Doughnut.'"

Since its humble beginnings, Voodoo has opened multiple locations in Portland, as well as bright pink stores in Eugene, Oregon; Denver, Colorado; Austin, Texas; and Taipei City, Taiwan.

Like Voodoo Doughnuts, the most beloved brands over-deliver on their RSP. The way in which you set up your culture and organization can make or break that promise. Hiring the best people who are in alignment with your mission and values are the best insurance against brand dilution.

2. **Think about your industry's weaknesses.** To figure out what you want to be the best at, start by taking a look at your industry: What are its weaknesses as a whole?

    For example, one company we mentioned earlier, Rackspace, is a website hosting company. For the most part, the industry deserves its poor reputation as a commodity with really poor customer service. People often choose their hosting provider solely based on price. Rackspace did something dramatically different by providing what they call "fanatical support" to its customers.

    That means:

    - Hiring Rackspace employees who are naturally inclined to serve.
    - A three-day-long onboarding process where new hires learn about the company's history and commitment to its mission.
    - Giving employees the freedom to do what they feel is best for the customer.

"Sometimes that means sending a customer a cake on their birthday or reminding them that they need to send their mom flowers on her birthday," said Julian Lopez, Rackspace's director of customer loyalty, in an interview. "Or, that means spending four hours on the phone with a customer troubleshooting on Thanksgiving or Christmas Eve. Our customer service comes in many forms, but when a customer comes back and gives us a ten out of ten on our net promoter survey, that is how we know we've succeeded. For us, that is the equivalent of a standing ovation."[35]

We think Rackspace is an interesting case study for two reasons:

- Their commitment to their RSP runs deep throughout their company and includes the people they hire along with their training process.
- They showcase an RSP that leveraged a sorely lacking component within the hosting industry: great customer service.

3. **Revisit your dream customers' pain points.** After you've examined your industry's weaknesses and determined where your company's opportunity to shine lies, revisit your target customers' pain points and the functional, economic, and emotional benefits you provide to them. From there, it's your task to create an RSP that unabashedly appeals to your dream customers.

Remarkability comes in many flavors. Depending on your industry and competitive landscape, your competitive differentiator(s) may be based on specialization, expertise, innovation, quality, commitment, replicability, customer service, delivery scope, delivery timing, accuracy, ease, convenience, location(s), expansiveness, uniqueness, customization, experience, breadth or depth of offerings, performance, quantity options, and/or your people.

Here are questions to help you develop your RSP:

- What do your dream customers really want?
- How can your offering solve their problem(s)?
- What motivates their buying decisions?
- Why do your existing customers choose you over the competition?
- What is your competitive advantage (i.e., what makes you remarkable)?
- What are you (or can you be) the best at that no one else in your industry is doing?

Set aside time for a brainstorming session to answer these questions. Then, narrow your concepts down until you come up with a single statement—one that lets your prospects and customers know what you deliver each and every time is remarkable.

Now, let's look at the second stage of building your Curtain Wall: your Service Delivery Map.

CURTAIN WALL PRINCIPLE #2:
CREATE A SERVICE DELIVERY MAP

A SERVICE DELIVERY MAP IS A SIMPLE CONCEPT: IT'S A set of steps (we like to pair it with a diagram) that explains the stages your customer will go through as they engage with your company. Developing a unique Service Delivery Map will help further your differentiation and systematize your offerings. More specifically, your Service Delivery Map will:

- Give order and structure to your delivery methodology.
- Ensure that all of the people in your company are in alignment with the way they serve your customers.

- Provide service that is unique to your brand but consistent throughout your company.
- Make training new hires simpler because they have a repeatable process to follow.
- Scale your services more easily as your company grows.
- Get the knowledge out of the leaders' brains (often the founders of a company deliver a service in a particular fashion, but because it lives in their heads, no one else in the company can replicate it).
- Improve the quality of your sales team's conversations by providing them a proven process that they can show and discuss with prospects.
- Enhance your conversion rates because people will be excited about your signature approach to service.

The approach Kinesis typically takes with our clients to develop their branded Service Delivery Map is to have them start thinking about the steps and actions that they are already taking, beginning with the point when they first start working with a customer—often this is some sort of assessment or research or investigation stage. Then what do they do next: how do they start implementing? Then what next? And so on, through each stage of service delivery until the final step.

When you think about developing your exclusive Service Delivery Map, consider what it means to sell your client the "full-meal deal" instead of a one-off project or even a phase of a project. If money wasn't an issue, what would bring them the absolute best value? When you think of the top decision-maker in the organization, what is bringing them the highest level of pain and what can you do to solve it?

Don't unnecessarily limit the scope of your projects. Let us explain. A lot of the companies we've worked with start with prospects by pitching the first phase as a stand-alone project—it's an evaluation or an assessment or an audit. This is a very typical approach for many service-centric organizations. The concept behind it is simple—the company pitches this investigation project as a foot in the door. Their belief is that they can sell a lower-priced project like this first, and then the outcome of their initial phase will lead to more work.

We believe this approach is flawed. Here is an illustrative example of this approach, which we find very common.

Let's envision an IT consulting company which we will call Bridgeworks. They typically provide a "foot in the door" assessment to review a client company's technology infrastructure to see if they have the right systems in place to meet new demands over the next three years. This IT assessment includes an analysis of their security protocol, people capacity, risk profile, and performance gaps. Let's say the business development person pitches and closes this IT assessment for $10,000 to a client company we will call Axis.

Bridgeworks goes in to Axis and performs its analysis. As part of it, they develop a strategic road map with a set of objectives that should be implemented in order to rectify all of the IT weaknesses that inevitably come out of the assessment.

The execution of this strategic road map with all of the indicated compliance measures, new technology infrastructure, risk protocol, and so on will take place over the next three years. It costs $150,000, which Bridgeworks hopes Axis will hire them to put into place.

This is a very typical approach in the B2B world. Start with an assessment, evaluation, test, beta period, etc., and then get paid to show the need for the larger scope of work. And, at first blush, it seems to make a lot of sense.

However, here's why we think this approach is errant.

Before Bridgeworks can execute the plan for Axis, their sales team must go *back* in front of the customer—often climbing the food chain within the organization to talk with higher-level decision-makers (because the middle managers who were able to approve a $10,000 project don't have the clout to approve a $150,000, three-year proposal of work). And then, the sales team has to pitch all over again—typically to a new set of people in the C Suite—to get them to sign a contract for the implementation as an entirely different project. They haven't developed a relationship with the true decision-makers because they've been working with the IT managers. In addition, they have a further barrier—the decision-makers don't really understand the complexities and rationale for the larger project, especially since they weren't interviewed as part of the assessment. The leadership's desired outcomes for the road map were not taken into account.

And, so the entire assessment project has been a low-priced entry into Axis that really hasn't brought the Bridgeworks team any true leverage (and most likely, very little profit). In our opinion, this additional pitching and ladder-climbing is a waste of time and effort—the entire package could have been sold to the right decision-maker(s) from the start and incorporated their desired outcomes from the leadership-level perspective. And—with a few additional value-added components along with the over-arching goals woven in—could have been priced at $250,000.

Here's why.

There's an old expression that says "Give a man a fish, he'll eat for a day, teach him to fish and he'll eat for a lifetime." However, in today's business world, we argue that neither of these approaches is applicable. Your client has no interest in fishing—that's why he/she is hiring *your* company for *your* expertise.

And while you could sell your customer a fish—which is often what happens when you sell that one-off assessment project to that middle-level manager—what many C-Suite executives *really* want is a fully-cooked, ready-to-eat five-course lobster dinner. If you can provide that level of value with an outcome that helps them to realize a higher-level leadership goal, they will pay you a premium—and it's often easier to sell when you present it as a package. Plus, you have very little competition because few companies understand this approach.

We advocate cultivating a relationship early on with the true high-level decision-makers and presenting them a comprehensive project plan that is framed by a Service Delivery Map.

Service Delivery Maps generally have four or five segments from Phase 1 to completion. Here are the steps we typically see:

STEP 1. Uncover the problem: Most companies typically start their Service Delivery Map with some sort of deep-dive research phase. This stage might be called discover, evaluate, assess, plan, identify, interview, ask, or define. During this step, you work with your customer to gather the requirements and define the process for the services you will deliver. You can brainstorm and set goals in this stage. It's essentially the assessment project that we described in the Bridgeworks example above, but using the Service Delivery Map, it's deliberately wrapped into the package and it may have a higher price point because it should deliver more value to the client company versus the traditional foot-in-the-door one-off assessment.

This phase should never be done for free as a proposal. You are in business to make money not undertake "spec" work. We have helped many of companies to move away from this paradigm—even when it's rife within their industry. Instead, sell this first phase to your customer letting them know they will benefit by having a customized solution that will deliver the best solution to their problem.

During this uncover-the-problem phase, we recommend you include interviews with a variety of stakeholders, as well as conducting research, implementing surveys, and so on. Typically both quantitative and qualitative elements will go into this initial phase. To provide the most value to your client, you should uncover the full scope of the problem that your client company is facing. This step is crucial to supporting the strategic thinking that will come in Step 2.

We also believe this phase should include regular meetings with the decision-makers, as well as mid-level managers. First, this is because it will give you better data. But the second reason is because you will develop cross-departmental, up-and-down-the-chain relationships that will help to position your company as a partner within the organization and increase loyalty with a variety of team members. This strategy helps your company become enmeshed with your client's organization and avoids the pitfall of having only one point of contact. In our experience, the single-point-of-contact relationship is efficient for getting work done, but presents a tremendous risk to the long-term customer relationship.

STEP 2. Chart the course: Next the Service Delivery Map process moves on to some form of on-the-ground investigative work. For instance, you could call this step analyze, map, blueprint, propose, define, construct, or build—in other words, you're in the pre-implementation phase.

During this phase, you are creating a comprehensive strategic road map or detailed plan that lays out the scope of work that will solve the problem(s) you uncovered in Step 1. This map can include insights, recommendations, goals, and planned actions. In the Bridgeworks example above, this is the three-year strategy for IT implementation that they developed as part of their assessment for their client, Axis.

STEP 3: Set it in motion: This is the implement, execute, launch, perform, accomplish, or act stage. At this point, your plan is in action and your team is carrying it out in the client company. You are following the road map you developed in Step 2. This phase could last weeks or months or years, depending on your industry or the scope of the project or the complexity of your services.

STEP 4: Measure your results: In this final stage, you'll be doing some form of evaluation to determine the success of your implementation phase. Other names for this step include: evaluate, measure, track, quantify, gauge, monitor, or learn. Ideally you have metrics associated with this step to quantify the success of your solution.

STEP 5. Rinse and repeat recommendations: After the final phase of your service delivery map, we typically suggest you have a formal process that you include on your Service Delivery Map. If you've done your work correctly, you should have new recommendations that come out of the large project you have just implemented that add additional value to your customer. These new recommendations lead to more work for you.

The reason for this rinse and repeat component is two-fold: (1) If you weave high-level stakeholders into your process, then they will discover the value you can bring to the organization and will often hire you to solve another problem and (2) You want to extend your relationship with your client into a multi-year buying cycle.

So the key to success with this approach is to be able to sell the value that your company can provide to your prospect with your entire phased project.

To succeed in this approach, you have to be willing to tolerate a longer sales cycle because it takes a while to get to the true decision-makers. You also must be willing to help the mid-level managers develop a strategy to champion your company and services to their bosses. They will often be the ones who find you for a simpler project (like the assessment), but when you position your services correctly using the entire scope of the phased project, you'll need to go to the vice president level for approval—and they can help you get there.

When you are pitching to high-level decision-makers, make sure that you sell them on the value and the return on investment of the entire project. You may find that they still want to break it into phases of implementation and payment, but because you have pitched and sold the entire scope to them, you won't have to resell them on each component, especially if you involve multiple stake-holders in your delivery.

In addition, include clauses in your contract in case your client requests additional work that is outside the scope of your proposal. This will happen, so plan for it.

Here's an example of a Service Delivery Map from a financial planning firm:

1. **Research:** Our team gathers your financial information to determine how we can best deliver value to you.

2. **Plan:** Using our financial planning tools, we map out how to best align and manage your assets.

3. **Implement:** Our team works with you to ensure your financial goals are translated into meaningful action that secures your future.

4. **Evaluate:** Our team will meet with you regularly to review your goals, plans, and taxes. We'll work with you to update your portfolio and match your evolving needs.

5. **Review and adjust:** Our team will facilitate a "review and adjust" period at the end of each evaluation where we work with you to adjust your goals as your lifestyle and life events shift (examples might include: child is born, child begins college, new home, retirement, divorce, etc.).

No two of our clients' Service Delivery Maps have ever looked the same, although they all have a lot of similarities (as we described above). We offer these examples to inspire you to create your own road map based on our overarching methodology, combined with your unique RSP and the specific needs and those of your customers. The key is to have a basic process that you can work through again and again—the steps you choose should be unique and in alignment with your brand.

Creating Your Own Service Delivery Map

Now think about your own Service Delivery Map. Can you break your process down into four to five big-picture steps? Begin by listing the major actions of every job or project. Then once you have identified the high-level steps of your Service Delivery Map process, it's time to begin carving out the details.

Document the specific actions required for each component. For example, your first step might be to *"Uncover the Problem"*—a phase that may consist of the following steps:

- A kickoff meeting with all stakeholders.
- Individual interviews with each stakeholder.

- An internal team meeting to debrief.
- An analysis of the strengths, weaknesses, opportunities, and threats (SWOT) of the issue you were hired to solve.
- A report that you share with key decision-makers.

Each of these steps offers an opportunity to fortify your curtain wall. What branded tools can you create to deliver each step? Can you carve out additional differentiators that none of your competitors offer? For instance, perhaps you can create a unique assessment tool that you deliver to each stakeholder. Maybe you have a unique model for forecasting that you can turn into an online or mobile application.

CURTAIN WALL PRINCIPLE #3: PRODUCTIZE YOUR SERVICES

ABACUS IS A CPA FIRM WITH AMAZING EMPLOYEES WHO provide exceptional services—and, as a result, they enjoy a high customer retention rate. In an industry characterized by high client turnover, it is noteworthy that the average customer has stayed with Abacus for fifteen years.

They've also perfected a marketing and sales strategy to attract many of these clients. When they first came to us, they had about fifteen hundred clients. Of these, 56 percent were veterinarians, 19 percent were medical practices, and the rest came from a variety of other industries. At that time, their average vet-clinic client spent $6,000 with the firm each year; and the average tax-only client spent $525 per year.

But it was obvious that they had not yet built a clear curtain wall to truly differentiate themselves.

Like most accounting firms, Abacus billed its clients by the hour with "a-la-carte" service offerings. But they discovered their clients were often using other firms for their personal returns and/or were hiring a separate bookkeeper. They also suffered from high levels of write-offs (money that they thought their clients wouldn't pay to them) due to inefficiencies and clients sometimes not being able to afford all of their services. This was seriously hurting the firm's profitability.

To help Abacus capitalize on its incredible strengths (excellent customer service, high customer retention, vet-clinic expertise) and minimize its weaknesses (lower paying clients, per-hour charges, write-offs, minimal profitability), we helped them differentiate themselves and productize their services.

The first thing they did was to stop accepting anyone who wasn't a dream customer (willing-to-pay-a-premium vet-clinic clients). This allowed them to develop a brand as *the* go-to accounting firm for veterinary practices.

Next they completely restructured their service offerings so they were no longer offering a-la-carte, per-hour services. Instead, they began to charge an annual fee of $7,500 for a package that included financial statement preparation, accounting system implementation, bookkeeping, personal and business tax returns, payroll services, litigation support, and practice management—everything that a vet-clinic owner needs to grow his or her practice.

Now, when the Abacus sales team talks to prospects, they are able to talk about their package—they take a uniquely proactive approach to accounting and none of the competition can provide the same depth of services or specialization.

Abacus also has a branded Service Delivery Map methodology that they share with new accountants and consultants who join their team so that they can continue to scale with ease. Their leadership team has multiple templates and checklists to ensure that each employee delivers service using their standardized approach. And by packaging their offerings, they've made it easy for their veterinary clients to spread the word about this company.

Because of the work they've done, the company can predict their cash flow since they are paid up front by their clients, and in turn, their clients have an easy way to plan their expenses for accounting and consulting. There are no surprises.

By productizing their services and switching to packaged deals, they've not only been able to skyrocket their revenue and profits, but they have a waiting list to become a client because their reputation as being remarkable in their niche has become so well known.

Why you should productize your services

Services are intangible. You can't photograph them, hold them, or hand them to a customer. Services are also hard to scale and they're risky—it's hard to estimate the scope of projects, which often results in low estimates.

Productizing your services makes the intangible, tangible. This puts customers at ease for a few reasons:

- Productizing makes the services seem more "real." Establishing a fixed price reduces their fear of runaway costs.
- You also are demonstrating you have a proven process to give them the outcome they want.

But it also has profound benefits for your business.

Typically customers pay for services after the work has been delivered. Even with simple transactions like haircuts or plumbing work, you pay service providers after the work is done.

In other words, customers have been trained to pay for your services after they receive them. This puts your organization at risk by delaying cash flow. Sure you may be able to get a down payment but, by and large, you are only going to receive your money after services are rendered. You run the risk of receiving only a partial payment—or worse, no payment at all. This will only happen in rare instances, but if the invoice is large enough, this can cripple a small- or medium-sized business.

In contrast, when you productize your services, you can define payment terms differently. By documenting the unique product you are offering, you can charge a fixed fee upfront. This increases your business' cash flow and working capital which, in turn, increases the overall value of your company.

Productizing services also allows your company to make efficiency profitable. As your team becomes more skilled and efficient, in a "bill-per-hour" approach, your company actually gets dinged for getting more skilled. You can do it more quickly, so you get paid less? That doesn't make any sense at all. Sure you can increase the rate that you charge for a senior-level professional, but you don't want them doing everything. It would be better if they focused on the high-level thinking and your more junior people (who cost you less) can work on the lower-skilled components of the project.

Consider the following scenario involving a public relations firm. If it takes one of the firm's newer junior associates 4.5 hours to write and edit a press release at $150/hr plus another 30 minutes for a senior associate to edit it (0.5 hours @$250/hr), the client is charged $800 for the release. On the other hand, if a more experienced—but still junior—associate can quickly write the release in just 2 hours with 30 minutes of review and editing from the senior associate, the client is charged about half that. In this model, junior staff are trained at the client's expense. And the agency makes less despite a more experienced staffer handling the job more efficiently.

In contrast, let's say this agency has productized this service:

writing a press release has a set price of $700. If that organization has well-trained staff who become experts at writing press releases quickly, then the agency sees more of that $700 as profit as efficiency increases.

Your sales team will also have an easier time selling your products. Instead of having to always say "Yes, we can develop a proposal for that" and then spending hours on writing up the proposed project (with no guarantee of getting the work), they can say "Oh yes, we have a solution for that. It's called XYZ and let me tell you about several success stories from some of our other clients."

When people hear you already have implemented a similar solution, they are more likely to convert into a paying customer because you are more positioned as the expert. Plus your business development people no longer have to spend hours and hours developing a non-paid proposal.

You can often create variations of your product. The easiest approach is to add products together. You may have your core offer (give it a name) and then you can add on other productized services such as assessment + core offer + training on core offer. All of a sudden, you can easily convert your prospects into larger ticket customers from the start.

Where to begin?

If your company provides customized services or experiences, you may not view them as processes which can be easily repeated and turned into products. However, that's exactly what they are—you just have to break each process down into its core components. At the moment, an understanding of those components—and their true value—may only reside in your founders' heads. Let's get them documented! Here's a step-by-step approach to productizing your services:

1. **Make a list of all the services that you offer.** Once you have listed each service, eliminate all of the ones that can't be broken down into steps and aren't teachable to employees. As the leader of your company, you can't be the only vault of knowledge. If you can't break a single service down into steps, you may have to combine services into the ideal offer.

   The Los Angeles-based Concierge Medical provides a good example of the power of packaged services. The company offers three levels of membership service—basic, standard, and advanced—each with a monthly fee. Among the basic and standard services included are walk-in and evening visits, valet parking, personal physician email access, and prescriptions called into drugstores.

   The deluxe level includes 24/7 access to the physician's cell phone, vaccinations, pap smears, weight loss programs, x-rays, blood tests, physical therapy, and an annual presidential physical almost identical to the one the physicians provide to the United States president.

   As members, patients enjoy the benefits of having easy and ongoing access to their doctors. They don't have to feel like they are part of the factory shuffle that is the plight of so many of our United States medical practices and institutions. And they know that most of their annual medical expenses are covered under their monthly dues—they don't have to wrangle with insurance companies and pay unforeseen high deductibles.

   By packaging their services, Medical Concierge is experiencing some amazing benefits that the typical provider does not. Each month, they realize an influx of membership fees before they pay any payroll or other expenses—they do not have to wait months for payment from insurance or Medicare. Based on their membership numbers, they can predict their monthly and annual revenue and adjust their operations accordingly.

2. **Narrow the field.** Once you've determined which services are teachable to other team members, then narrow the field further by identifying those services that are the most profitable, valuable to your customers, and in demand. From the final contenders, choose one service to productize first.

3. **Break it down.** Now comes the hard part—you must take what's in your brain and break it down into repeatable steps. (Not only will this help you develop a roster of product levels, but it can act as the training manual that you can use to teach your employees exactly how your company delivers X, Y, and Z.) Once you have all of the steps written down, have a team member read them to see if they don't understand an area. Keep revising until it is easy to follow.

   As we mentioned, documenting your process for service delivery is not easy. Most service providers have developed a unique way of delivering their offerings that has evolved over time. The steps have become intuitive to them and, as such, are not easy to break into discrete chunks that can be repeated by others.

   Expect to go through multiple drafts—and keep in mind that the components will change over time. When Kinesis first started our retainer-based approach, we called this productized service the "Growth Program." Over time, our philosophy evolved, which led to the development of our Marketing From the Inside Out® approach. Getting it right will take patience and perseverance—but the payoff is well worth it.

4. **Next, develop pricing for your offering.** This is the fun part! You get to move away from the dreaded (and often money-losing) billable hour and toward a fixed fee that your client will pay for upfront. To get to the appropriate pricing, look at similar past

projects that were profitable. Develop a ground-level pricing plan and then make sure you add enough into the productized service so that you can provide effective assessment, project management, and implementation in addition to development.

Founded in 2009, Wealth Enhancers (WE) specializes in serving Generation Y, a vastly underserved niche in the financial planning world. They have productized their offerings and offer services to both individuals and business clients.

At the time of writing, they have two levels for business clients: the WEgrow at $18,000/year and the WEpartner at $30,000/year. Their package includes a goals and vision session, quarterly coaching, financial reporting, business insurance, human resources, and more.

For the individual, they have three packages each associated with a one-time payment plus a monthly fee and all named with a WE branded moniker: Activate, Achieve, and Advance. Their packages include financial advice, cash flow management, insurance recommendations, portfolio management, estate planning, and more. By branding and packaging their offerings, WE lets prospects know exactly what they will be receiving for their selected package.

The owners of the company started as two people in 2009, but as a result of developing productized services, they were easily able to train additional team members. In just five years, they have become an award-winning organization with three locations and more than twenty employees who deliver the same consistent service.

5. **Have a plan for scope creep.** We recommend placing contingency plans into your contracts so that you will get paid if your client adds to the scope of the work of your productized

service (scope creep). If it is helpful to your company and the way in which you deliver services, consider developing a phased approach to the work (just be sure to sell an agreement for all phases upfront). This is where the Service Delivery Map can be helpful.

6. **Develop a memorable name for your offering.** A name not only differentiates your service/product from the competition, it also gives you and your team ownership over it. The name ties it into your company brand. In addition to naming your productized services, you can create unique names for your proprietary tools, processes, applications, methodologies, and so on.

   At Kinesis, we've developed several unique tools and pro-cesses such as our Metric Dashboard™, Marketing Blueprint™, and unique approach to annual strategic planning sessions.

   A name and visual representation of your productized ser-vice will pique the interest of your prospects and help them con-nect more deeply with it. It will also make it easier for people to talk about your offering with their peers. And there's nothing like word-of-mouth recommendations to send people flocking to your door.

7. **Systematize your progress updates.** As you begin to productize your services, also consider the steps that you can take to keep yourself top of mind during the delivery. You can systematize check-in points that keep you in front of your clients on at least a weekly basis. By making yourself a part of their rhythms, it becomes a lot easier to sell the next productized service. Prog-ress updates and deliverables that help you stay top of mind can include:

- A weekly phone call
- Meetings with stakeholders at key junctures
- A weekly email progress report
- Well-designed slide decks giving a visual representation of your results to date

The good news is: once you have productized one service, it becomes easier to do the same for additional offerings. And when you start to get your brain out of the way as a barrier to scaling your company by documenting and systematizing your services, you'll be surprised at how eager your employees will be to learn your system and then deliver it in your signature method to your customers.

Differentiation is one of the most important strategic and tactical activities your company has—it's an ongoing process in which your company must constantly engage. By turning the intangible elements of your approach into concrete products that people will talk about, you will create an impenetrable fortress around your business.

Remember, while it may feel risky to be remarkable, being mediocre is a far greater risk.

BUILD A THOUGHT PLATFORM AROUND YOUR REMARKABLE IDEAS

"Thought leaders are brave; explore areas
others don't, raise questions others won't,
and provide insights others can't."

—Craig Badings and Liz Alexander, authors
and leadership consultants

GIVEN THAT WE'RE LIVING IN THE AGE OF THE TED TALKS, you've no doubt heard the term *thought leader*. However, there are a lot of different opinions on what it means. So let's make sure we agree on the definition before we go any further.

As we see it, a thought leader is an informed, go-to person in her or his field of expertise. They are trusted sources who move and inspire people with their ideas and opinions.

If you think about it for a few minutes, I'm sure you can think of multiple thought leaders who attract a lot of attention. They may be in your industry—or they may be in a different field altogether.

They could be an author, speaker, blogger, TV celebrity, or all of these things! Think about the Suze Ormans, Malcolm Gladwells, Herminia Ibarras, and Elon Musks of the world.

People seek out thought leaders because of their knowledge, expertise, and savvy. One of the ways you can spot a thought leader is that they seem to be "everywhere." They are asked to speak at conferences, events, and they are interviewed on radio shows, podcasts, and on TV broadcasts. The press loves them—and they themselves write for the best publications and have thousands of followers on social media.

What all thought leaders have in common is that—because of their visibility and perceived authority—their companies or platforms attract people as if by magic. People love spreading the word about their ideas, services, and products. It's been years since they've made a cold call and they don't need to spend a lot of money on advertising. People chase *them* down to pay for their advice, not the other way around. And, unsurprisingly, they command premium fees for their services. These individuals have worked hard to build an audience of raving fans and now they are reaping the benefits of this work.

While we often associate thought leadership with individuals, businesses, too, can adopt a thought leadership marketing strategy.

There are several large consulting firms that have been at the forefront of this company-wide thought leadership approach. Companies such as Deloitte, PwC, Accenture, Bain, IBM, and McKinsey have long understood that taking the time and making the effort to leverage content created by multiple individuals to demonstrate the company's expertise is well worth the effort.

While individual thought leaders like Elizabeth Gilbert, Gretchen Rubin, and Tony Robbins act as the faces of their platforms and companies, sustainable thought-leadership marketing for small- and medium-sized businesses functions better as a system when it is not reliant on a single person.

Rather companies who take a thought leadership marketing approach employ people we at Kinesis refer to as "Concept Champions."

Concept Champions are those individuals in your organization who can help to build your curtain wall. These individuals exemplify your mission and values. They have a foundation of subject matter expertise and a positive, knowledgeable reputation as a trustworthy expert. There are a number of different ways that you can leverage different people as Concept Champions. We'll dive more deeply into this in a moment.

And even if you have a charismatic leader (most likely your CEO or a founding partner) who will act as a key Concept Champion, we encourage you to create a company brand as a thought leader. Develop and nurture multiple Concept Champions who can become spokespeople for your organization.

Here's what a thought leadership marketing strategy that leverages the skills of your Concept Champions can help you achieve:

- Attract a large audience who can ultimately become customers and/or refer you to potential customers
- Extends your curtain wall so you increase customer loyalty and raise your average customer lifetime value
- Increase your company's ability to get featured by the press, enabling you to increase exposure
- Engages your potential buyers into a relationship with your organization that increases their likelihood of becoming a customer
- Adds credibility to your company and shortens the buying cycle
- Improves your sales effectiveness

- Attracts your right-fit prospects
- Positions your company as one led by visionary thinkers
- Kills your competition by showcasing your unique way of solving problems

One of our clients, Powers—a commercial contractor—has an innovative and forward-thinking CEO at the helm: His Big Vision is a company that produces zero waste and holds itself to the highest environmental standards. This vision become part of the company's differentiation since Powers' environmentally minded approach is very unusual in its industry. We helped them create website content, downloads, blog posts, and marketing materials that tout their commitments and accomplishments in recycling, reclaiming, and reusing materials.

And their sales team uses these assets as part of their sales process. They talk about Powers' novel approach when they are at networking meetings with prospects. They follow up with emails with links to website and blog content. In short, the sales team has become masterful at leveraging the company's position as a thought leader.

As a result, over the last three years, Powers has won large contracts with very prominent clients. This is something that the company would have never dreamed about just a few years ago. But Powers' large corporate clients have fairly strict environmental policies; by hiring Powers, they can better uphold their commitment to sustainability. A win-win all around.

Their success would never have happened without implementing a thought leadership marketing strategy. These days, the sales team doesn't have to do much prospecting because Powers' reputation has grown enough through word-of-mouth marketing that the sales team is now primarily focused on closing contracts—a good position to be in.

Start your thought leadership marketing efforts by thinking about the people in your organization and beginning to identify potential Concept Champions. You can begin with your natural networkers, leaders, teachers, and writers. There are many ways you can begin to implement your thought leadership marketing strategy by leveraging your Concept Champions' strengths.

For instance, at Kinesis, we've identified Concept Champions who love online networking. Several of us have already developed our own followings on LinkedIn, Instagram, and Twitter. We leverage this by distributing blogs posts and other Kinesis content through these individuals on their social media channels in addition to our company profiles. This is an easy way to leverage our people's existing networks to get multiple eyeballs on our content.

Other individuals at Kinesis are amazing in-person networkers. These Concept Champions connect with prospects at targeted events and give presentations at conferences. Finally, we have several people who are fantastic writers. These Concept Champions contribute to our blog.

To orchestrate our Concept Champions' efforts, we have developed a thought leadership plan with specific dates, goals, and themes. This gives us control of our messages and content. Our internal marketing department sets and executes the overarching thought leadership strategy so that all the Concept Champions are on message and in alignment with our brand.

While this is one way to leverage the people in your organization, don't worry if you don't have charismatic speakers and networkers in your company. We understand that some industries attract more "behind-the-scenes" types. But even organizations filled with introverts can still build a thought leadership marketing strategy by getting creative about how individuals can use their unique skills to become Concept Champions.

The bottom line is: elevating the visibility of multiple people in your company increases the visibility of your brand. Regardless of the types of personalities within your organization, you can develop Concept Champions—as long as you think creatively about your people's given strengths and passions, and consider what your dream customers want to see, read, watch, and experience.

For an example of a less conventional approach, consider the strategy of one of our clients—Sharp Inc., a nine-person company that specializes in software training and support. Their team is made up by a lot of technically brilliant people who, unsurprisingly, aren't running out the door to give a TED talk. Their people don't like small talk or networking, they aren't chatting up people at conferences, and no one in the company would ever define her- or himself as an extrovert.

While working with them to develop a thought leadership marketing strategy, we noticed that one member of their team, Bob, gives amazing online demos. His enthusiasm and passion for the business excites and engages audiences online. Bob also reaches potential dream customers by contributing answers to various tech forums.

We saw an opportunity for Sharp to gain notoriety and authority by building a Concept Champion plan that started with Bob and eventually wove in other programmers and engineers.

As multiple people in the company became Concept Champions, Sharp's thought leadership marketing strategy revolved around posting software training/demo videos on their blog as well as leveraging them into on-demand webinars. They posted these same videos on a YouTube channel, and then began to regularly post on Facebook, LinkedIn, and Twitter. By appointing several Concept Champions and connecting their work to an overarching thought leadership marketing strategy, and implementing consistently, Sharp has increased the demand for their software consulting services and installation expertise.

The owner of another tech company, Scope, was an incredibly charismatic extrovert who loved to speak, write, present, and network. The rest of his company? No thanks. They preferred to spend their weekends decompressing, playing online games. So we capitalized on the CEO's passion for getting out in the world. He created blog posts, flew all around the country for events, developed webinars, filmed videos, and is even finishing up a book!

Now I know most of us don't have that kind of energy, but this guy does! So we leveraged his passions and as a result, his company's growth has been astronomical. Recognizing the tremendous value he provided as the primary Content Champion liberated him to put other people in charge of sales, account management, and all the programming and analysis that served their customers.

While appointing an incredibly charismatic leader to the role of Concept Champion is a no-brainer, we urge you to seek out as many different Content Champions as possible. The reasons for this are simple:

1. If a person leaves your business or wants to focus on other activities, you can continue to move forward with your thought leadership marketing. Your organization won't be severely impacted because you were hanging your hat on their network and efforts.

2. Small- and medium-sized businesses have a harder time carving out enough time for a single person to produce enough content to rise above the noise and get your company noticed as a thought leader. With more Concept Champions, you can generate more content.

3. You have multiple people in your organization who have amazing skills and areas of expertise. By elevating them to Concept Champions, you not only increase their enthusiasm and engagement in your company, you also offer your audience different perspectives.

4. Focusing only on your senior leadership (who are incredibly busy) narrows the number and depth of topics you can explore. It also limits the types of content you can produce and the channels you can distribute it on.

5. Your brand is more powerful and more remarkable when it is actively represented by a diverse, fluid body of voices. Each Concept Champion's voice adds depth, resonance, and power.

Kinesis, Sharp, and Scope have all taken three very different approaches to thought leadership marketing.

The next section will help you develop a plan that is best for you and the personality of your company.

STEP 1: Assess: The first step in creating a thought leadership marketing strategy is to understand where you are right now, along with the unique strengths you can leverage. Here is a series of questions that will give you the foundation of the Assessment step.

First, assess gaps and issues in your industry.
Ask the following questions:

- What are other companies and industry experts overlooking?
- What does our company offer that is unique within our industry and why is it a better solution?

- Do others in our industry have a "right" way to do things that we disagree with? If so, why?
- Is something in my industry "broken" that needs to be done differently? If so, how does it need to change?
- What trends are coming down the pike and how can our company help our clients prepare to thrive? How will these trends change my industry?
- What innovations/unique approaches do we know about that others do not?

Assess your company's brand, people, and dream customers.
Ask the following questions:

- What ideas contribute to our curtain wall that we can champion as part of our thought leadership marketing strategy?
- What people do we have in our company who can become Concept Champions?
- What are our potential Concept Champions' strengths and how can we best leverage them?
- What are our potential Concept Champions currently doing that we can build upon?
- What are the personalities of our potential Concept Champions and what platforms would align the best with their styles, approaches, and voices?
- Where are the places/events/online platforms where our Concept Champions can reach our dream customers?
- What do our dream customers want?
- What do our dream customers value?
- What do our dream customers rely upon our organization to solve?
- What questions do our dream customers frequently ask us that we have a unique take on?

You may discover that the answers to these questions are already integrated into the solutions that you provide to your dream customers. Or you may find that you have more work to do to get enough clarity to develop a body of work around your concepts.

The good news is that you've already begun by completing the work in the previous chapters. You've defined your dream customers and you understand their pain points. You know the core benefits you provide. You've created your RSP, outlined your Service Delivery Map, and begun the process of building your curtain wall. These are all assets that will contribute to your remarkability, your unique brand, and your differentiation. They can be woven into your thought leadership marketing strategy.

Assess your current level of visibility.

Your next step is to determine your current level of visibility and what needs improvement. The following questions will help you:

- Are we already writing about our Service Delivery Map, productized services, and related concepts on our company blog?
- Do we have a presence on any social media platforms? If so, how big is our network/following?
- Are we posting regularly to our social media channels with links back to our website and blog?
- Do we have existing relationships with the media? How about industry blogs/publications?
- Are we actively growing and nurturing relationships with the media, industry event organizers, and centers of influence in our field of expertise?
- Do we have strategic partnerships with synergistic organizations that we can comarket with to grow our audience?

- Is our company offering webinars, presentations, and/or workshops on our signature methods and related concepts?
- Do we have multiple people from our organization who are creating content for our blog, website, and social media?
- Does our website highlight our productized services and Service Delivery Map?
- Do we have position papers that elucidate elements of our unique approach and productized services?
- Is there a speakers' page on our website?
- What relationships do we currently have with industry influencers?
- Could our current clients describe what makes our company remarkable and are they connected to us online?
- Do prospects choose us based on our remarkability?
- Do our marketing materials and sales team talk about our remarkability, productized services, and Service Delivery Map?
- Are we attending key industry events? Are we positioned to speak at them?

In addition to answering the questions in the list above, take time to write down your key areas of strengths and weaknesses when it comes to promoting your productized services, Service Delivery Map, and related concepts. Make a list of the marketing channels you are currently using, along with the ones you *could* be leveraging. You may find you are already actively promoting across marketing channels. Or you may identify multiple places you need to have a presence. Regardless of where your company is right now, write down everything you are currently doing and then note everything you *could* be doing.

STEP 2: Plan: Once you've assessed your current marketing visibility and communication, it's time to jump into planning mode. We recommend scheduling a series of thought leadership planning meetings where you flesh out the different activities we describe below.

As we mentioned above, the first thing to do is to is to designate your Concept Champions. Pick people who have different strengths and insights that are fresh, relevant, and intriguing. This means they will stay abreast of what's going on in your industry and with your customers. They are enthusiastic contributors and are committed to continually learning new skills and deepening their expertise. If you are brand new to thought leadership marketing, then you may want to start with just one or two people, especially if you are a smaller company.

Next, consider what your ideal customer wants when you are creating this content. A study by the CMO Council found that 87 percent of B2B buyers said online content has either a major or moderate impact on vendor preference and selection. The characteristics they most value? The breadth and depth of information and originality of thinking and ideas.[36]

Identify the activities you must take on as an organization to promote your blog and other online marketing assets. We recommend starting by ensuring that the pages on your website are fleshed out with your core services, and then adding a resource area on your website with position/white papers, articles, and videos. Your next step would be to develop a blog if you don't already have one.

To plan content, we like to use an editorial calendar that—at the very least—has dates, content topic, person responsible, and the place where it will be posted. Of course, this can be a very simple planning tool or you can get quite complex depending on the needs of your organization.

Keep in mind when you are developing this calendar that regularity matters. For instance, if you already have a blog but only post sporadically, consider being more strategic about how you plan the publishing frequency in your editorial calendar—we recommend posting every two weeks to start and weekly if you are more ambitious.

Next determine what social media platforms you need to leverage to reach your dream client. Then develop a social media calendar that lists the platform, promotion dates, and person responsible. Also consider how you can get more power out of each platform. For example, if you are on LinkedIn, ask yourself:

- How can we create a regular schedule to seek out new strategic alliances and post updates about our core ideas?
- What can we do to update our LinkedIn newsfeed and drive people back to our blog?
- Which Concept Champions can update their newsfeed regularly with content about our organization and industry?

Your calendars should be a shareable resource that your Concept Champions and marketing team can use to plan your content activity. It allows everyone to visualize how you will distribute your content throughout the year. You can also plan content around key events or important dates (for example, an accounting firm may want an entire series of blog posts leading up to Tax Day). It also serves as a tool to keep your Concept Champions accountable to deadlines.

To keep everyone on track, you should designate one person to oversee the editorial calendar (this person needn't be a Concept Champion, but they should be organized). She or he can track the calendars and remind Concept Champions of upcoming deadlines, nudge people to get their tasks done, and schedule promotions to social media and your blog. This person can also hold a regular meeting about the content that you are creating—depending on your organization, these meetings can be monthly or quarterly. This planning time can also be used for updating and revising your editorial calendar as you progress.

Another of our clients—a law firm called Jones & Blacke—was frustrated when they first started working with us because only a handful of their partners and attorneys were networking and bringing in new clients. Their goal was to spread the efforts across almost all of the more than twenty partners and attorneys in the firm (especially their newer hires).

As part of our planning phase, we developed a strategy for them to bolster their LinkedIn profile in order to have a greater impact on their commercial clients. Next we designated Concept Champions who were knowledgeable in their respective areas of expertise such as construction litigation, cyber law, medical malpractice, and environmental law. We also developed an editorial calendar that had a targeted blog post going up every two weeks—authorship was shared so there was not an excessive burden on any one individual.

Additionally the firm wanted to help newer attorneys learn better networking and sales strategies to help them grow their own book of clients. So we developed a strategy that involved revamping the monthly all-team meeting: the networking, sales, and blogging "rock stars" in the firm would spend an additional fifteen to thirty minutes training the other partners and attorneys in their best practices.

The final part of the plan involving empowering several members of their administrative staff to plan monthly meetings, remind people of their blog deadlines, and plan networking events. The administrative staff members also were responsible for tracking their numbers on a scorecard we developed for each attorney.

STEP 3: Implement: Once you have your thought leadership marketing strategy in place, it's time to begin implementing your plan. One of the most important things to keep in mind is: consistency counts! You want to get in front of your dream customers again and again and again. So stick to your editorial calendars!

List of assets

You will find that there are many ways to continue improving during the implementation phase. Below is a list of assets that many of our clients enhance as part of their thought leadership marketing strategies:

- **Bolster your "About" page.** Your "About" page is typically the first place new visitors to your website will review after they've scanned the home page to learn more about your company, philosophy, and differentiators. Make sure that this page is amazing and builds interest around your unique services. You can include links to other places on your site you want visitors to see.

- **Consider an "Our Approach" or "Why Us?" page.** This gives you an opportunity to describe your unique differentiators and espouse your core concepts. Adding information (bios, key links) about your leadership or team page boosts credibility.

- **Make your pages searchable.** If you optimize your blog posts and website pages for online searches, this will bring more people to your website. In their survey of more than four hundred B2B marketers Salesforce/Pardot found that 78 percent of B2B buyers start with a Google search.[37] This trend provides you with a great opportunity to reel in new fans who will embrace your ideas.

- **Nurture leads via your website.** Offer more premium content—reports, guides, white papers, screencasts, and webinars—in exchange for a visitor's name and email address. This will allow you to build a list of interested prospects that you can notify when you have a new asset and, over time, you can build an extensive library of online content.

Build your platform

If you are going to share ideas through your thought leadership marketing activities, you need someone to listen and watch. As part of your implementation, you should work to build and nurture a loyal audience of leads, customers, and business supporters who are interested in your ideas. Here are some places to focus your efforts:

- **Build and nurture an email list:** Most of the B2B companies we work with are pretty far behind the business-to-consumer (B2C) world when it comes to building and nurturing an email list of customers and prospects. They often don't see the need. But an email list is important to any company. Even if you sell to businesses, there is still a person making the decisions about whether to hire your company—and that means there's a relationship to be nurtured.

  Building and marketing to a list is an inexpensive method for regularly communicating with your customers, prospects, referrers, and business connections. You can keep people apprised of updates in your company and, most important, stay in front of your network so that your company is the first one that comes to mind when they need a service that you are providing.

  Start your list by entering the names and emails of your organizational contacts—as well as people you meet at networking events, associations, and via mutual business colleagues. This

176

can be a very effective way of expanding your subscriber base—but make sure you ask people if they would like to be added to your list. If you don't have people's permission, it's a violation of the CAN-SPAM Act (this is the law that establishes requirements for emails used in business—other countries have similar laws to protect consumers).

Keep in touch with your list on a regular basis—it's crucial to send out regular email content to your list that is of interest to your subscribers. Our favorite mechanism is the email newsletter. Newsletters keep clients engaged and aware of your company and its offerings. You can include industry news and trends, legislative updates, business tips and tricks, and educational content. Always ask yourself, "How can I provide more value to my dream customers?"

You can also send out targeted email campaigns for a host of different purposes—educating your audience, offering services, promoting a special, launching a new offering, and so on. One benefit of having a regular newsletter is that your audience won't be surprised by a campaign—you've already gotten them accustomed to receiving emails from you on a regular basis.

Stick to your editorial calendar to keep track of your blogging schedule and topics, hold Concept Champions accountable for writing posts, and pinpoint date-specific events that could relate to your content such as holidays and conferences. This strategy makes it easy for you to nurture relationships with your network.

- *Tap into personal circles*: To begin expanding your company's platform, encourage Concept Champions to start with their personal circles. We've found that in the firms we've worked with, our clients' employees have been excited to take this on, so don't be afraid to ask your staff members.

Below are some ways to harness and grow each Concept Champion's network:

Have each Concept Champion make a list of her or his personal network: prospects, past coworkers, current and previous customers, business friends, referrers, contractors, online connections, and/or vendors. Essentially, the list should include everyone the person is connected to in his or her professional life. Then break down the lists into categories to help prioritize who to reach out to first.

Next ask each Concept Champion to send out an email to these individuals telling them about what you are doing in your organization and inviting them to download one of your assets. The email should include a link to a landing page on your website—create a box where they enter their name and email to get the asset. Let people know somewhere on this page that by giving their email, you'll be adding them to your e-newsletter list. Then in the first email to them, get their permission to send additional content. Also ask these new subscribers to share the landing page and asset download with people they know who may be interested. There are also widgets you can install on your website to make this easy.

Your Concept Champions can also share the links to your landing pages (with the downloadable assets) with their network via social media channels—LinkedIn is certainly a powerful platform for B2B and professional connections, but depending on your industry, you may have other social media channels or forums that are relevant. For example, we have a couple of clients who build custom LEED-certified/green homes, commercial buildings, and developments: the social media site, Houzz, is a great way for these clients to reach out to their prospects as well as partnering companies such as architects, interior designers, consultants, and subcontractors.

- ***Get industry famous***: Now it's time to get your Concept Champions out in the world. Here is a list of ideas to get you started (there are some that will appeal more to extroverts, and others that will be more suited to the introverts in your company):

  - Networking and speaking at local events
  - Speaking at national trade/industry events
  - Writing articles for trade/industry print and online publications
  - Being interviewed for a trade/industry blog, podcast, MeetUp, radio show, or article
  - Hosting webinars for an online association—they provide the platform and marketing, you provide the core concepts
  - Hosting events at your facility
  - Designing infographics that illustrate your core concepts
  - Cohosting events with a synergistic company and comarketing to your lists
  - Being part of a panel with other influencers
  - Creating press releases every time your company does something newsworthy
  - Writing a book about your core concepts (it's easier than ever to self-publish)
  - Recording videos and/or screencasts and posting them on a YouTube channel
  - Creating slide presentations around your core concepts and posting them on SlideShare
  - Getting on stage for a local TED talk
  - Asking your network to share your content

It can take time to gain traction with your efforts, so don't feel frustrated in the first few months. Stay consistent with your plan and keep pushing your ideas and resources out in the world. Over time, your efforts will begin to snowball.

For example, in 2010, software company Wild Apricot leveraged LinkedIn to boost their thought leadership marketing. They first created a LinkedIn company page and then encouraged their existing customers to post recommendations and reviews. They increased the frequency of their blog posts and began posting regular links to these posts on their company pages' newsfeed.

"We started reaching out to customers who had given us feedback by email or our customer survey," said former vice president of marketing, Jay Moonah. "Any time we respond to feedback, we include a link to our LinkedIn page and encourage people to post reviews—we do this in our newsletter as well."

They were quickly able to get twenty-five recommendations which they highlighted on their website. Conversion on their home page rose 15 percent.

The company has continued to implement a thought leadership marketing strategy: As we write this in early 2017, Wild Apricot offers many different webinars and online courses for their audience. They now have thousands of followers on multiple social media sites and were ranked the #1 Membership Management Software by the software review site Capterra. More than sixteen thousand organizations now use their software and they've grown from thirty employees in 2007 to more than one hundred today.

- ***Get locally famous***: A lot of marketing experts assume that every company is trying to reach a national client base—and so, they'll share one-size-fits-all advice that has worked in global power-houses with a huge reach. In fact, what we've found is that many of the strategies that work for the biggest players won't be of much help to companies looking to target a smaller, local geography.

  If a good chunk of your customers is based in one, or a few, areas, one of the most powerful thought leadership strategies is to make your business "locally famous." Even if you market to a much larger area (or are hoping to scale), you can use these ideas to build a strong base in your home area.

  This work is not difficult, but it will take focus, consistency, and commitment to build your company reputation locally. The great news is that very few of your competitors will be utilizing all of these strategies, so you have a huge opportunity to stand out.

Develop relationships with business reporters

Most cities have several local business journals whose reporters have realized that in order to survive, they must do two things: (1) Tell more stories about local businesses and (2) Shift all of their publishing efforts to the content-hungry internet.

Each day these reporters wake up and think, "What am I going to write about today?" This means that they need *your* expertise more than ever. Your Concept Champion (or the person helping to support him/her) can call your local business reporter and/or editor and pitch them your story ideas. You have things to talk about: like how you have a great culture and how you are weathering the current industry/economic/employment/whatever-the-latest-story-is.

Think of this as an ongoing sales activity. Your goal is to get reporters/editors excited about your ideas and your company. And don't get discouraged since it may take several attempts to get them on board.

Don't send ideas in the mail or via email. Lots of reporters like relationships—just like your more extraverted Concept Champions. So invite your local business editor and/or reporter out to lunch (if they can't make it, then take them coffee and donuts—yes, really!).

While you are chatting, ask them how you can help support their efforts. Examples of content or news they might be interested include: expert quotes, commentary about marketplace trends, interesting or troubling news in your industry or community, details about changes in leadership, job openings, interesting legislation affecting your customer base, and so on.

Remember, local business publishers have shifted their focus online. This means they are on an ongoing quest for great content. If you are an authority on a specific area of expertise, you or a Concept Champion may even be able to get a spot as a guest or regular con-tributor—an excellent way to get consistent free exposure.

Nominate your business and people for local awards and lists

Your local business publications, associations, and organizations have numerous awards and lists. Examples in our area include: 100 Best Companies to Work For, Orchid Awards (honoring top women business leaders), 40 Under 40 (recognizes younger high-achieving entrepreneurs), *The Portland Business Journal*'s CFO of the Year Award, Top Oregon Manufacturing Firms, and so on. The winners of these awards get lots of press when they win, and the opportunity to connect with other business leaders.

You can use Google to find out which local lists and awards are a good fit for your company and people. Then nominate yourself. Remember if you don't enter, you'll never win. Since it takes some work, this eliminates a lot of your competitors right off the bat because they won't have the motivation or time to put in the effort.

Network smart

Shop networking events until you find the right fit, then attend. While we're sure you've already considered networking as an option, what you may not have considered is that not every networking event is a good fit.

Your time is precious. Therefore you should commit to and attend only the networking groups that are going to allow you to meet your target audience. That's why we recommend shopping around for several months. Use Google and ask business friends for recommendations to great networking groups, and then attend a few a month to see if your key buyers are attending them. When you find the golden groups, then (and only then) is it time to dedicate yourself to regular attendance.

Creating a "locally famous" business as part of your thought leadership marketing strategy will encourage customer loyalty, boost referrals, bring in new business, and help strengthen your brand against competitors. These strategies are not costly, but they do require time and effort. But remember, you're not just bringing in leads, you're nurturing relationships and building your company's renown . . . and that's the kind of lead generation that will pay off for months and years to come.

STEP 4: Measure

> "What gets measured gets managed."
> —Peter Drucker

For B2B companies, thought leadership is a powerful way to drive awareness, increase engagement, and drive sales. However, the last crucial piece in any thought leadership marketing strategy is to put into place systems to measure your efforts. Without thought leadership metrics, you don't know which strategies are working well and which aren't.

Remember: different companies require different metrics. Below we will list some common thought leadership marketing metrics, but we encourage you to choose the ones that will best demonstrate your return on investment:

Brand awareness/reputation

Of course, it's impossible to truly measure how much people are thinking about your organization, but tracking increases in certain activities should give you an idea. These include:

Website/blog/online

- Unique visits to your website
- Average time spent on your website
- Website page views
- Most popular pages/blog posts
- Number of "brand queries" (direct searches for your company name) to your website
- Number of downloads of digital assets
- Traffic flow from a website page deeper into your site
- Return visitors to website/blog
- Online reviews/testimonials (track both positive and negative)
- Online brand mentions

Your goal is to track which kinds of online content are getting attention and which are not. If you notice people gravitating toward a certain kind of post or piece of information, create more of it!

Lead generation/closed deals

Your thought leadership marketing efforts should bring you more leads. Therefore, make sure to track some metrics that focus on lead conversions—things like:

- Number of calls and web form submissions (track where these came from so that you can match up which efforts are driving leads)
- Number of client meetings generated
- Number of requests for proposals/contracts
- Value of proposals/contracts given to leads
- Number of closed proposals/contracts
- Value of all new business won

Social media analytics

Each social media platform has its own set of analytics. It may be difficult to track the number of leads you are getting from social media since the funnel can be more convoluted. That said, other factors that can contribute to your return on investment (ROI) include:

- Follower growth
- Likes/post reactions and comments
- Reach
- Brand mentions
- Content shared/popular content
- Referral traffic to your website/blog
- Click-through rates

Email newsletter/email campaigns

The following metrics should give you a well-rounded picture of which of your newsletter and email campaigns are getting the best response:

- List growth rate
- Delivery rate (this should be above 95 percent—if it slips below, clean your list)
- Open rates (please note: open rates are notoriously hard to track due to differences in recipients' email client settings. Keep an eye on these, but don't obsess over them.)
- Click-through rates
- Sharing/forwarding rate
- Conversion rate (percentage of email recipients who clicked on a link in your email and took a desired action such as filled out a lead generation form)
- Overall ROI

Other metrics

We've listed many measurements which will be useful and encourage you to focus on ones you think will be most useful for your company. In order to further your company's reputation as a thought leader, you may want to track other activities such as:

- Events that your Concept Champions are attending
- Number of leads generated from events
- Conversions from leads via events
- Awards won
- Media mentions of your organization
- Referrals given
- Leads from referrers
- Conversion of leads via referrers

Systematize thought leadership

There are tremendous benefits to positioning your firm as a thought leader, and leveraging the power of your people by promoting them to Concept Champions. It does require consistent and diligent effort. That's why creating systems to manage your content and track its effectiveness is critical to your long-term success.

While you can certainly purchase software to track your metrics, you can also use a simple spreadsheet. The key is to create an ongoing process for measuring your thought leadership efforts over time.

Use tools such as your editorial calendar will help keep your team on track. Plug in detail-oriented administrative staff to keep your Concept Champions productive and on time. Regularly assess your efforts.

Maximize the winning tactics and minimize the lackluster ones.

PRINCIPLE #8

MINE THE DIAMONDS
IN YOUR BACKYARD

"The best advertising you can have is a loyal
customer spreading the word about how
incredible your business is."

—Shep Hyken, author and speaker

ONE OF THE FIRST THINGS MOST OF OUR CLIENTS ASK US
is "How can I get more people and businesses into our sales pipeline?
How can I generate more leads?"

Of course, this is a crucial conversation—every organization
needs effective marketing and sales tactics to bring in new customers. You *should* work to create multiple pillars of marketing that
result in *total customer growth*—an increase in new customers while
you retain and grow the accounts you already have.

Unfortunately, many business leaders focus *all* of their attention on seeking new customers with projects that are challenging,
time-consuming, and costly. They focus almost exclusively on new
leads, while opportunities to expand sales with existing customers
go largely untouched.

One reason for this narrow focus is because—let's admit it—lead generation is a seductive route to grow revenue. Acquiring new customers involves the thrill of the hunt and the close of the sale. You and your team may *feel* like a new customer makes your business more money simply because they require such a large investment of time and people power (even if the metrics don't support this feeling). New customers can energize your team and create a lot of initial work that keeps everyone busy and seemingly productive. As a result, new business gets all of the attention, while customer retention is largely left to chance.

Too many leaders looking "out there" for a solution to all their woes pour a large percentage of their marketing budget into advertising and purchasing cold lists, but next to nothing on marketing to existing customers or reconnecting with past accounts. In a 2014 survey by Forbes of top executives across the United States, only 38 percent of respondents said that their company is primarily focused on repeat customers for revenue growth.[38]

It's an error we see all too often, especially in service-centric businesses.

The High Cost of New Customers

In the early 1900s, Reverend Russell Conwell—American lawyer, author, and the founder of Temple University—gave a popular speech called "Acres of Diamonds." He delivered this inspirational talk more than six thousand times on a national lecture circuit. In it, he said: "Your diamonds are not in far distant mountains or in yonder seas. They are in your own backyard if you but dig for them."

In other words, you may have been seeking that elusive jackpot when it's been within your grasp all along. For business leaders, it's your network of relationships with your customers, your opportunities, and your leads. It's your partners, suppliers, and your centers of influence. It's the relationships that your employees have cultivated and the people who refer you time and again.

It is a huge oversight to focus most of your efforts on front-end sales in lieu of mining the diamonds in your own backyard. Why? Because the most profitable, inexpensive, and consistent revenue comes from the loyal customers who already know and like your company. Not only are they easier to sell to, but repeat customers spend an average of 67 percent more than a new one![39] (Compare that with the probability of selling to a new prospect: only 5 to 20 percent.) Retention is also a powerful profit lever. A mere 5 *percent increase in customer retention can increase a company's profitability by up to 75 percent!*[40]

What's more, according to one study, it's six to seven times costlier to get business from a new customer than an existing one.[41]

Why is the cost of new customers so high?

In almost all businesses, acquiring a new customer requires a big upfront investment. Whether you are using Google AdWords, direct mail, cold calls, or traditional advertising, it costs money to bring new prospects into your funnel—you need to factor in the cost of marketing (design time, copywriting, postage, materials, printing, and advertising fees) as well as internal staff time associated with learning about your new client and closing the deal.

This onboarding and ramp-up time will take its toll on efficiency and profit. In addition, new customers will not spend as much as existing customers because they are just getting to know, like, and trust you. Several of our clients have had to suffer through a "testing period" wherein a new account gives them a very small project to see if they like the relationship, customer service, and output. Their team members soon find themselves bending over backwards to make this new customer happy, with very little profit to show as a result—it's short-term pain for a long-term gain.

There is a better way.

Digging for Diamonds

After working with client after client on digging into their "diamond mine," we've identified multiple ways to uncover more opportunities from the relationships you already have:

1. *Focus on lifetime value, not transactional value*: Let's start by reframing the way in which you think about each customer.

Your first step is to understand your customer lifetime value (CLV)—in other words, the value that the relationship brings to your company over time, as opposed to during any one transaction.

A long-term relationship with a good customer is far more valuable that any one-time sale. In fact, the lifetime value of a customer can be astronomical, especially when you factor in the referrals and positive ratings from loyal customers along with their purchases of related services.

The various methods for calculating your CLV can be complex—with formulas created by graduates in finance and statistics. However, in its simplest form:

$$\text{CLV} =$$
$$\text{[the amount of time you retain a customer]}$$
$$\times$$
$$\text{[the average amount spent at each transaction]}$$
$$\times$$
$$\text{[the average number of transactions]}$$

Let's take as an example a mid-sized accounting firm—we'll call it ABC Accounting. Their average corporate customer stays with the firm for ten years and spends $5,000 each year for their taxes. Let's plug that into the formula:

10 years

×

$5000 average annual spend

×

1 transaction per year

= $50,000 CLV

To begin determining *your* CLV, you will have to analyze your data to figure out your average customer spend and your average customer retention rate.

To calculate your simple retention rate, take the number of customers from last year who are still customers this year. (If you have the data available, you can also track your retention over multiple years and take an average.)

If you want to add more data, begin to list the costs associated with your customers to determine their average profitability. Keep in mind that certain customers may demand ongoing discounts and a lot of time and attention from your team. Often these deep-discount types of customers are "cheap" to acquire but expensive over the long haul and probably not worth your time.

Once you have this basic CLV data, you can begin to make some decisions about your customers—in particular, which ones to keep and which ones to let go. As we discussed in Chapter 5, the best way to do this is to stratify your customers (remember our "5-Star Client" exercise?). As a reminder, we typically recommend a simple A, B, C categorization, although you may need to get more complex depending on the industry you are in and the types of services your company provides.

Once you've finished your stratification, look at your customers in your A list. What is their average annual spend? Most of them will be spending more than your average customer. And the top 15 to 20 percent of your list will be spending considerably more. Conversely, the bottom 20 percent of your customers will be high maintenance and low profits—they are expensive to retain.

Recall the Pareto principle we introduced earlier: roughly 80 percent of the effects come from 20 percent of the causes. In other words:

- 80 percent of your profits come from the top 20 percent of your clients.
- 80 percent of your revenue comes from the top 20 percent of your clients.
- 80 percent of your complaints, inefficiencies, and problems come from the bottom 20 percent of your clients.

Armed with this information, consider the top two-thirds of your A-level clients: your best, cream-of-the-crop, VIPs, special-sauce clients.

Take a moment to write down the reasons that your A-level clients are spending more, as well as the services and products that they are purchasing. You can use the following questions as a starting point:

- Why is this client spending with us repeatedly?
- Why is this client spending more with us?
- What services is this client using each year?
- What is the value that we are providing to this client?
- Why is this client so profitable?
- Who in our company is managing this relationship and what are they saying to the client?
- How is this client to work with? What do we really like about them?

Let's return to the ABC Accounting Firm example. While their average customer's annual spend is $5,000, when the leadership team looks at its best A-level clients, it discovers that they are spending around $9,000–$12,000 per year, which is significantly more than the average.

When the ABC Accounting team writes down the services and products the A-level clients are purchasing, they notice that these companies are not only having their corporate taxes done by the ABC, they are also requesting personal tax accounting for their CEOs and partners. In addition, they are hiring ABC for tax planning, consulting, payroll, and bookkeeping. In short, the company's best customers are using them for *all* of their financial needs.

You likely have similar clients—it's your job to identify them and give them the best possible treatment. Your company can improve dramatically by focusing on your customers with the highest CLV and eliminating the rest.

2. *Create a culture of sales*: Once you are armed with the information about *what* your A-level clients are buying, now it's time to look at *how* you are selling your services and products—and *who* is doing the selling.

Harvey MacKay, founder of MackayMitchell Envelope Company says that when people ask him "How many salespeople do you have?" he says "five hundred"—the exact same number of employees in the company.

"To me, job titles don't matter," he says. "Everyone is in sales. It's the only way we stay in business."

Think about that idea for a moment: every one of your employees who comes in contact with your customer can make or break the relationship. So why not create a culture of sales?

Your *entire* team must be able to up-sell and cross-sell your products and services. It has to come from every department. We are sympathetic to those of you who are thinking "I will never be able to get my [*fill in your resistant department*] people to sell."

We're here to tell you that you can! We've had many clients who have managed to integrate cross-selling and up-selling into their entire culture. It's simply a matter of creating processes for educating customers throughout the course of your engagement—which brings us to the next "digging for diamonds" strategy.

3. *Create a process for educating people about your offerings*: Make sure all of your offerings are included in your marketing materials—but you *also* need an ongoing process for educating your prospects and customers about your offerings.

Most companies don't have systematic sales or account management processes that allow their customers to know the entire breadth and depth of their offerings. As a result, employees often make the assumption that their prospects and customers understand everything they offer.

If your company is guilty of this common mistake, then your next step is to examine both your sales and client onboarding processes:

- How can you help new customers understand the full suite of services and products that you provide?
- How can you make older customers aware of them?
- How can you put systems in place so that different teams and divisions can up-sell and cross-sell your offerings?

A great place to start is during your initial needs analysis meeting (Step 1 in your Service Delivery Map). As you uncover your customers' goals and pain points, you may immediately find that in addition to the service they have already purchased, there are more items that you can add on to solve their issue.

During the onboarding process, don't forget to ask if there are other stakeholders or department representatives in your customers' company you should meet. Broadening your relationships with your client organizations can be an easy way to generate more revenue.

Implementing a company-wide system for informing your clients about the depth and breadth of your offerings is a powerful way to mine your diamonds. When developing your system, simply think about all the times you come into contact with the customer: how can you be sure to use each opportunity to educate them about how you might better serve them?

We often get push-back from our clients who tell us "We don't want to be perceived as a pushy company by our existing clients." We suggest they reframe their thinking: by offering additional services, you are helping your customers. After all, they have hired you to (1) alleviate a pain they are feeling, (2) provide value, (3) become an ongoing partner, and (4) act as a trusted resource.

If you are not telling your customers about the full breadth of services that you could provide to them, then you are actually doing them a disservice.

4. *Listen to what customers are asking for*: What are your customers asking for? The team at New York video company Sizzle It had gotten a number of inquiries from clients who wanted them to store their media files.

"They got in a habit of re-editing their sizzle reels several times over the course of a year," said Scott Gerber, the CEO of Sizzle It. By charging monthly and annual fees to store client video data, the company created a new recurring revenue stream.

Every time you add a new offering, don't forget to include it in your system and make sure to inform all your customers and prospects.

Hopefully, you already can see how each of the previous four strategies will help you mine the diamonds in your backyard.

Now take a look at your own customers. Are any missing out on the true value of what you provide? Are you listening to your customers to see if there are other services you can provide that they want? How much money are you allowing to go to other companies when your loyal customers would prefer to work with *you* if only they knew the scope of additional services you are able to provide? Plus you know your competitors—and their weaknesses—would you trust your business to them? Then why are you letting your clients?

You never want to hear "Oh, I didn't know you did that!" from your customers. Don't assume that the existence of your website and other marketing materials means your prospects and customers know about your full array of services.

It isn't up to them to figure it out or to remember. It's up to *you* to let them know.

CHANGE HOW YOU SELL TO PROSPECTS

WHEN WE START WORKING WITH MOST CLIENTS, THEY TYPICALLY have a "single transaction" sales approach. In other words:

- A design agency creates a logo or a brochure.
- An analytics firm provides a single service.
- A management consultancy administers a strategic assessment.

You get the idea. This approach has serious pitfalls. First off, you risk serious cash flow issues. In these types of transactional sales, a company typically does not get any cash until after the service is delivered and the customer receives an invoice. This means that employees are getting paid to do this work from your company coffers *before* any receivables have arrived. That's risky. There is also a chance (slim though it might seem) that you may never get paid or only get partial payment.

In addition, it's a one-and-done deal. Unless you have a carefully-planned sales cycle, your customer will pay you (if all goes well) after the work is completed and then go on their merry way. Now you have to wait until they think of something else to hire you to do. Even if you pitch them again, you'll need to put time and energy into the sales machine. Either way, it may be month or years until they re-hire you.

By rethinking your sales approach, your scenario could be much more lucrative, increase your customer retention, and add more value to your customers.

Consider the following two strategies:

1. ***Package your offerings for maximum value***: What we're going to tell you might make you uncomfortable so take a moment to sit with it before you react. Ready?

   It's as easy to sell a $100,000 package as it is to sell a $10,000 project.

Sounds weird, right? Let us explain how this works (and how packaging differs from productized services, which we discussed earlier). Packaging services is a pricing strategy popular in the retail industry: grouping several products together to create a more competitive price point increases cost efficiency and maximizes profit. There are many ways that retailers bundle products, including:

- **Restaurant:** several food items are put into a single package with a drink. Happy Meal, anyone?
- **Camera store:** A camera is bundled with accessories like an SD card, a light, a case, and a tripod.
- **Garden shop:** Mother's Day gift includes several flowering plants already potted in a vase.

Many B2B companies have also embraced the strategy.

One of our clients develops software and custom applications for other businesses. Fred, the company's CEO, was struggling because his customers weren't purchasing enough of his services to truly solve their problems.

But customers did have a request. They wanted a dashboard that would help them better understand and improve their sales process. The problem was, Fred and his team knew the clients' problems went a lot deeper—a dashboard alone wasn't really going to help them.

"All the sales or IT manager cares about is a 'sexy,' nice-looking dashboard that shows results," Fred explained.

Now when Fred really thought about it, he knew that the vice president of sales would probably be well aware of the systemic problems in their data mining techniques. But he couldn't convince the mid-level folks he did business with to understand the deeper problem—and potential solution.

As for his attempts to reach the C-Suite? "It almost always ends up being a dead end," he said. "The mid-level folks don't have the clout and they are often in a silo. Even if they do champion us, they don't have the knowledge to sway the executives."

But it wasn't just a problem of getting in the door (or getting in the right door).

Fred's company *also* lacked a package of services that would truly meet his clients' needs. Fred knew the real problem and the real solution, but because he wasn't talking to the right person and marketing his offerings successfully, he was stuck selling the one-off project—one that he knew wouldn't really help his clients.

It's a story we hear from clients all the time: They're simply not talking to the right buyers: the people who are really feeling the pain, the decision-makers who can truly see the value of a large-scale solution, the C-Suite execs who control the big budgets.

How do you solve this problem?

Fred and his team created several productized service offerings (*see Principle 6 for more on this topic*) and then bundled them together as one package. He changed his selling approach to integrate discussions with the key C-Suite decision-makers. When he was called by the mid-level manager who simply wanted the flashy dashboard, he was able to tell them that as part of his process, he needed to talk with multiple stakeholders during the assessment phase. (First, however, he would get the mid-level manager's input and incorporate it into his package.)

Because the new solution solved systemic problems (and included the pretty dashboard), it was easier to sell—even though the cost was five times as much as the one-off project. It made all the key stakeholders happy and provided real, long-lasting value.

As a result of selling a package, Fred could set a fixed fee that was paid before each phase began and that included a contingency for extra add-on services. Once he got his team working with the customer, they were able to generate even more work, because they were on the lookout for new sales opportunities. They made sure to ask poignant questions and bring up additional service options that could help the customer with more pain points. What once would have been a $10,000 dashboard project turned into a $100,000+ package. The customer's CLV skyrocketed.

How can package your own offerings differently? Can you string together an assessment process with a core service? Or tie together a distribution offering with a production element? Can you bundle several productized services? Think about what the higher-level decision-makers need to solve their biggest problems.

2. ***Add a subscription-based selling model***: There's nothing new about the idea of subscriptions: newspapers and magazines have been using this model for ages. Recurring revenue is the best kind: it smooths out your feast-or-famine cash flow cycles, allows you to confidently invest in onboarding and technology, and helps you more accurately predict revenue and spend way less energy and resources scrambling for the next job.

Recurring revenue also allows you to improve the relationship with your customers much like leveraging the Service Delivery Map and packaging services does: you improve your CLV, work with clients longer, and cater to their evolving needs.

Excitingly, the subscription model has exploded in recent years. There are Wine of the Month packages, Netflix streaming services, and the Dollar Shave Club sends you razors and creams for a few bucks a month—and the list goes on and on.

But B2C doesn't have a monopoly on subscription services. Many service-oriented companies are turning to recurrent revenue models as well. Take, for example, goBRANDgo!, a St. Louis-based marketing firm.

"In 2014, we had some months when we billed more than $150,000 and some months when we billed $80,000," recalls Brandon Dempsey, managing partner. "These swings in revenue cost us virtually all of our profit; we were often paying for people to sit in our office without anything to do."[42]

The company moved exclusively to a subscription-based model, and now charges a flat-recurring rate each month.

"Monthly recurring revenue (MRR) is predictable and enables good accounting and cash practices in business," Brandon says. "It has helped us to dramatically drive profitability and allows me to sleep much better at night. It changed our business almost overnight and provided a foundation that continues to grow stronger. Before this billing methodology, we were struggling to stay afloat. Today we have two months' payroll in savings and a large amount of cash flow so we can have a lot more fun."

Another example is One Medical, a health-care company who partners with employers to offer a bundle of benefits such as same-day appointments, more personal treatment plans, and direct access to doctors outside the office—patients can talk with providers via video and phone conferencing. ThriveWorks is a similar type of business, but it provides counseling services and life coaching for a small monthly membership fee.[43]

Over the past few years, the growth strategies for B2B businesses have opened up radically thanks to subscription-based services. In part, this is because people have gotten used to this model as a consumer, so doing it for their company makes sense as well. This is especially true because the software they are using for sales and project management, marketing automation, and accounting have all shifted to an ongoing monthly payment system (think about QuickBooks, Salesforce, Basecamp, Hubspot, and Asana to name a few examples). This model has proven so successful that many of these software-as-a-service (SaaS) companies are pulling in multi-billion dollar valuations.

In addition, technology makes it easier for your customers to connect directly and continuously with your service company. For example, customers can set up automated payments via direct debit, access a customer service representative, complete a service request form, or look up service information via your website.

To help you determine how your company can embrace subscription-based selling, let's look at some additional examples from the B2B world.

1. **Retainer-based model**: At Kinesis, we shifted from our early one-off project shop to a retainer-based model. Now clients pay us a fixed fee each month for their basic agreed-upon services plus any additional project work they request. To sell retainer agreements, make sure your prospects know that your firm is in demand—your team requires a retainer to allocate the internal resources of your team and to maintain and support the work you've already completed (if applicable). Options to sweeten the retainer agreement with a customer might include a discounted rate and/or an exclusivity agreement (i.e., your firm won't serve direct competitors of your client).

2. **Access to proprietary information + consulting package:** A consulting company can create a proprietary software that helps their business clients calculate or manage a process. The company can begin to package an offering that includes access to the software along with consulting services for a monthly fee. This type of business could also, for a monthly fee, allow customers to retain its consulting services when needed (this model has long been used in the legal industry).

3. **Service + upkeep packages:** An organization that provides a skilled trade such as commercial plumbing or landscaping or cleaning or IT can offer monthly maintenance contracts that provide ongoing repairs and upkeep for the monthly fee. This can be upsold to customers when they call for upgrades, installation, or repairs.

4. ***Bundled packages***: An accounting firm could package services such as business tax returns, owners' tax returns, tax and financial advice, and audits and then amortize them over a year so they turn their fee structure into a subscription-based model. It would even out the accounting firm's cash flow and their clients' output. Plus their clients will be more likely to ask them for ongoing assistance and advice under this structure because they aren't worried about getting hit with extra bills. It's a win for both parties.

These approaches provide additional advantages to your customers. First, they enjoy the auto-pilot simplicity of knowing that they don't have to think about payment or budgeting—your fixed fee is a set-it-and-forget-it cost that they can allocate each month. They also get peace of mind from knowing that your business is there for them to provide the assistance or maintenance they require. Tie in a subscription-based service with packaging and your customer enjoys extras simply for being one of your preferred subscribers.

Ask yourself:

- What services might you provide to clients on a subscription-based basis?
- What bonuses can you also package with your core offerings?
- How can you leverage this type of system?

Another thing we love about subscription-based pricing: No more speculative work, zero proposals, and much less pitching. What could your organization accomplish by freeing up all of those hours that your team is currently spending on these activities? Could you make your services even better for your existing customers, further increasing their loyalty and happiness? Think about the possibilities!

MINING YOUR NETWORK OF CUSTOMERS AND REFERRERS

NOW THAT YOU'VE DONE SOME THINKING ABOUT INCREASING the lifetime value of each customer and developed bundled packages, a subscription-based model, or some hybrid of these approaches, it's time to really dive into your network and share what you have to offer.

Contact past customers

Do you have a system in place for regularly contacting past customers? If not, you are missing some diamonds in your backyard. Think about the people and companies who already have a good relationship with your business—and remember that it's up to you to keep them abreast of service updates. Here are some ways to start the conversation:

- Talk to them about your new productized services, packages, and retainer-based offerings.

- Offer them Step 1 in one of your Service Delivery Maps such as an audit, analysis, or evaluation of an aspect of their business that might need a "tune up."

- Call or visit them to talk about recent projects that are relevant to them. Use this as the starting point for your conversation: "We just finished up a project that I thought would be interesting to you, so I thought I would get in touch."

- Talk to them about recent news and industry developments, new legislation or regulations, or updated technology. And be sure to ask them about what's changed in their business—their answer may give you a chance to tell them about how you can help them with your services.

- You can also contact past customers to gather feedback. Even if you don't do more work with them, the answers to these questions can help you develop stronger connections with your network and learn important things about your dream clients. For example, ask them "What's the biggest problem facing your business?" or "What's one thing that none of your vendors do that you wish they would?" or "As you look ahead to the next year in business, what are you most excited about?" There are many poignant questions that will help you improve your offerings, so consider what questions will help your organization the most.

Think about all of the ways you can provide value to your past customers. You can also share this same information with current clients to further nurture the relationship. If you have a sales force, your team members will love this "non-sales" sales strategy. They are always hungry for reasons to connect with people.

Sometimes even the simple act of reconnecting leads to new business. We had one client who called a list of past business clients to simply say "Hello, it's been a while. . . . How are things? Here's what I've been up to lately." By making just twenty phone calls, our client got contracts for $686,000 in new work. Now those are some big, shiny diamonds!

We had another client company in the skilled trades that decided to increase the number of maintenance contracts. They armed their salesperson with some reports and articles to share with past customers. While he was meeting with them, he described their updated service maintenance contracts and made sure his contacts understood the value of regular upkeep. In just a few months, he landed hundreds of thousands of dollars in recurring revenue from multiple past clients.

You can make your diamond-mining efforts even more powerful by systemizing them. This shouldn't be a one-time endeavor. Instead, you should be regularly connecting with past clients. Make a schedule for everyone in your organization that interacts with clients. Whether it's once a quarter or once a year, create a process and make sure to regularly implement it.

Ask for referrals

You're probably already aware of the power of referrals. It's no secret that word-of-mouth referrals are among the top ways professional services firms get leads and new business.

A study published by the American Marketing Association[44] found that peer recommendations are 2.5 times more responsive than any other marketing channel. And a 2011 study published in the *Harvard Business Review*[45] found that referred customers generate higher margins and higher retention than other customers, making them more valuable in both the short and long run.

So why do so many companies miss the mark when it comes to getting referrals?

In order to excel at driving business through referrals, a business must do two things:

1. *Be referable: Offer amazing service.* Adding value and delivering on client expectations provide the foundation for word-of-mouth marketing. Even the most robust referral system won't generate results if you can't offer an outstanding customer experience.

2. *Develop and implement an effective referral program.* Once you've refined the customer experience piece, then creating and

practicing an effective referral program can have a major impact on your bottom line.

Systematizing your referral program is key because too many companies believe that providing value and amazing service to their customers will automatically result in referrals with no further effort on their part. Unfortunately, great service is not enough to get a flood of referrals.

If you do not ask for the referral, you are not likely to get it. It's not because your clients don't want to give one. It's more likely that they are busy and your company is "out of sight, out of mind" unless you are there to remind them.

Below we've outlined the main steps to creating a referral system and suggestions for putting it into practice. Remember every business is unique, and your system will need to be tailored to your industry practices and marketing strategy.

STEP 1: Target your dream customers (and your dream referrers): Targeting the right people is essential for the success of your referral system. A deep understanding of your dream customers makes it easier to describe your perfect prospect to referrers.

Then, identify your "dream referrers"—the people who know your company and already think highly of it. Typically, they have some sort of pull on your prospect, either through a personal or working relationship. Referrers can be existing clients, vendors, complimentary service providers, and/or business friends.

STEP 2: Educate referral sources: Once you've identified your referrers, equip them with the right tools. Make sure your referrers understand how your company is unique and how your products and services make a difference to your ideal clients. Your referrers should also know who your dream clients are.

Equip your referrers with valuable content they can share with their networks. Reports and guides can be easily passed along—either in person or via email. You can also help your referrers connect you to others on the internet. Make sure to update your LinkedIn profile and LinkedIn company page so your referrers can provide online introductions and make connections virtually.

STEP 3: Ask for referrals: We understand that asking for referrals can be intimidating. You may worry that your client will think you're pushy or rude. Rest assured—after many years of consulting with a variety of different companies in a myriad of industries, we have only seen positive responses from polite, professional requests for referrals.

Begin by developing a methodical system to ask for referrals from your clients. Ask for referrals at key points in your customer relationship. You can also include "referrals appreciated" reminders in your email signature, newsletter correspondence, and on your website. This is a good option if you have a broad base of referral sources that you reach out to on a regular basis. If you have forms that you deliver to customers on a regular basis such as receipts of payment, this can be another place to print this message.

Be sure to incorporate referral language into your client appreciation materials. Not only are you nurturing your client relationship, you're asking for referrals in a more intimate, less invasive way.

STEP 4: Recognize your referrers: When you show your referral sources that you appreciate their support, you're ensuring their continued enthusiasm for sharing your message.

There are many ways to recognize your referral sources.

Simple correspondence is effective and affordable. Make a phone call, send an email, or—better yet—send a handwritten note to express your appreciation. Because most people have forgotten about the good ol' handwritten note, you'll stand out by writing one.

Giving gifts to referrers not only recognizes their efforts but encourages additional referrals. Send a gift card, or grant them discounted products or services to express your appreciation when one of their referrals converts.

Depending on your industry, you may want to consider incentivizing referrals for key relationships. Certain companies have relationships with the sales reps of complimentary software or types of services. There is often an opportunity to explore a formal spiff arrangement. This approach definitely isn't for every company, but we've found it does work well for certain sectors. You can also incentivize customer referral from your employees.

STEP 5: Measure referral marketing efforts: In order to leverage your referral system for the best results, it's critical to track your referrals and analyze key metrics. With the right amount of measurement, you can answer questions like:

- Who are my best referral sources?
- How does my referral conversion rate compare to my overall lead conversion rate?
- What's the ROI for my referral system?
- How can I refine my referral system for a greater ROI?

Incorporating these elements into your marketing strategy will put you on track for an effective referral system that drives business and makes you more profitable. You can also tie it into your customer relationship management (CRM) software so that your sales team is sure to input sales made as a result of referrals.

The first time you ask a client or partner business for a referral, you may be nervous and it might be awkward. Just keep in mind that you are asking people who already trust you and know what a good job your company does. Your customer wants to see you succeed and will not be annoyed by your request.

So what are you going to do to mine the diamonds in your backyard? How can you start leveraging your network of relationships? From calling past clients to creating subscription-based selling models to up-selling existing accounts, you have a plethora of options to begin to expand your opportunities. Start with one of the techniques listed in this chapter and begin planning the steps to implement it throughout your company. Turn it into a repeatable system that is part of your regular operations.

Then move onto the next facet of your diamond mining. Rinse and repeat until you have many ways to grow the revenue from your existing network.

NURTURE YOUR CUSTOMERS INTO RAVING FANS

"Customer service shouldn't just be a department, it should be the entire company."

—Tony Hsieh, CEO of Zappos

WHILE ATTENDING A COCKTAIL PARTY IN NEW YORK, EDITOR in chief at 1to1 Media, Mila D'Antonio, met a flight attendant who'd just flown back in from Costa Rica—she'd driven to the party straight from John F. Kennedy International Airport, in fact. When Mila asked her which airline she worked for, the flight attendant replied, "The worst airline in the world."

"Let me guess," Mila said. "United Airlines."[46]

Her guess was right. Sadly, the company was *that* notorious for poor customer service. If you look at all the performance metrics from 2012 to 2015—delays, cancellations, mishandled bags, bumped passengers—United has been reliably the worst or near worst of all the airlines. As for the 2015 J.D. Power and Associates customer satisfaction survey, it finished last among North American non-discount airlines.[47]

"United is off-the-charts worse than anything I've ever seen," says Lenny Mendonca, a retired senior partner at McKinsey. Despite having flown more than three million miles with the airline, he says, "If I have any other alternative, I will fly with someone else."

Yes, United was hated during this period. And also really bad at leveraging social media. This was unfortunate, because United's customers were not. Between 2012 and 2015, the five major airlines saw a 209 percent increase in mentions on Twitter. And United was one of two airlines with the highest rate of negative posts—a whopping 56 percent.[48]

In 2012, an article reported that the airline ranked below industry average on many social media metrics, such as interactions, response time, and Twitter followers.

Several of the negative interactions have become cautionary tales about how *not* to act in the age of social media: when United charged social media expert Peter Shankman $50 to fly standby on an earlier flight than the one on which he was booked, he complained on his Facebook business page to his forty-seven thousand friends—122 liked his post, 39 took the time to comment on it, and still more learned about the story when it came up in their feeds.[49]

But that doesn't compare to the fallout that occurred when a singer named Dave Carroll was flying United with his band members from Nova Scotia to Nebraska, with a layover at Chicago's O'Hare International Airport. As they were waiting to deplane at O'Hare, Dave overheard another passenger exclaim: "My God, they're throwing guitars out there!"

As Dave and his bandmates looked out the plane windows, they saw the luggage—including their instruments—being vigorously unloaded. He immediately tried to communicate with the flight attendant who cut him off and said: "Don't talk to me. Talk to the lead agent outside."

But the lead agent refused to talk to him. And the third United employee Dave approached dismissed him, saying, "But hun, that's why we make you sign the waiver." (There had been no waiver.) When the band finally went to retrieve their guitars from the baggage unloading area in Omaha, Dave found that his lovely $3,500 710 Taylor guitar's neck had been broken.

He says he tried making numerous phone calls and emails to try and get United to reimburse him for the damage. He even asked for flight vouchers instead of money. Each time, United told him no.

After nine months of fighting with United, Dave did what a singer-songwriter does best—he wrote a song about the experience called "United Breaks Guitars." Then he uploaded it to YouTube. He asked his friends to Tweet it and share it on Facebook and eventually the video was picked up by news sites and bloggers, becoming a viral sensation.

One hundred fifty thousand views in, Dave finally got United's attention. They called to offer payment to make the song go away. Unfortunately for United, Dave had discovered that he liked writing songs about his broken guitar (and the attention he was getting as a result). He went on to write "United Breaks Guitars 2" and "United Breaks Guitars 3," then wrote the book *United Breaks Guitars: The Power of One Voice in the Age of Social Media*. Dave became a sought-after guest on many radio and TV shows—he did more than two hundred interviews in the first few months on major news media including ABC's *20/20*, *Rolling Stones Magazine*, CNN, *Wall Street Journal*, and BBC to name a few.[50]

As of writing this sentence, the video has 16,304,951 views.

Unfortunately, United Airlines seems to have learned little from this incident about customer service. In 2017, another social media firestorm swept around the world when United passenger Dr. David Dao was physically ejected from a plane because the flight was overbooked (and, by "physically ejected," we mean, "punched in the face").

"Had United shown compassion and intent to make things right, they could have come out of this at the very least looking like an airline that cares," said public relations expert Ed Zitron. "Instead they've just made it even worse."

While these are certainly big, dramatic stories, United's poor customer service are hardly isolated events in businesses. And it certainly isn't something that is only relevant to certain types of industries.

What's particularly important for businesses to understand is the power that consumers have to make public commentary about the companies that treat them well—and those that don't.

The 2000s saw the explosion of what is known as the "Sharing Economy." Thanks to the social web, you can share anything with anybody—whether it's loans, ideas, building plans, houses, cars, clothes, couches, apartments, tools, meals, and even skills. Another major factor driving this trend is the rise of Millennial influence—not only is this generation tech-savvy, they love to share their thoughts on just about everything.

Customers of every company—including yours—are sharing texts, photos, videos, but more than anything, they are sharing their opinions. And not only do they share information, they also seek it out. The financial collapse of 2008 and the subsequent Great Recession has made all consumers more careful researchers.

Unsurprisingly, the battered consumer emerged from this crisis more cautious and more discerning. Where once people may have spent with little thought, many have adopted a more frugal "save-for-the-rainy-day" mind-set. When Americans do spend, they are vigilant in making sure they get the best value for their hard-earned money. And the information is out there—if someone can't find a review on Yelp, Rotten Tomatoes, Trip Advisor, or YouTube, a buyer can just ask their friends on Facebook or Twitter or LinkedIn.

Meet the modern customers: They're heavily networked, highly connected—and they care about what their online friends have to say. They are cautious researchers, seeking out recommendations, reading online reviews, and carefully considering their options.

These trends are evidence of shifting behaviors in consumers— and not simply in the B2C space. Almost all consumers—depending on which study you look at, it ranges from 85 to 97 percent—use the internet to research products and services before making purchases. And Acquity Group's annual *State of B2B Procurement Study* reports that 84 percent of B2B buyers do online research before making a purchase.[51]

The same user-generated critiques that have affected the consumer brands are becoming increasingly prevalent in the B2B world. After all, your business customers are consumers too. Ask yourself— how did *you* make your last electronics or car or appliance purchase? What did you do before you purchased your most recent book or saw the latest movie or ate out at a new restaurant? If you are like most of us, you went to a site and read some peer reviews.

And, of course, these same consumers are the B2B purchasers that your company wants to become your new customers. And their personal habits and their business habits online are all spilling over into one another.

As a B2B company, the stakes are even higher because the average purchase is so much larger. Your prospects expect you to be the expert, working hard to earn (and keep) their dollars, and they want to feel good about your brand. From the moment they first hear about your company, they have begun to assess whether or not they believe you can get the job done.

Every touchpoint matters.

Despite all of these shifts in buyers' behavior and the new marketing ecosystem, the leaders of many companies—especially smaller B2B companies—are not responding to the realities of today's marketplace quickly enough. Too many companies are not staying ahead of the curve and acting proactively by delivering the best customer experience they can provide. Even if you have the best, most sophisticated product, if you have terrible service people will remember and they will spread the word.

"Even the best of what formerly passed for good customer service is no longer enough," wrote Gary Vaynerchuk in *The Thank You Economy*. "You have to be no less than a customer concierge, doing everything you can to make every one of your customers feel acknowledged, appreciated, and heard. You have to make them feel special, just like when your great-grandmother walked into Butcher Bob's shop or bought her new hat, and you need to make people who aren't your customers wish they were. Social media gives businesses the tools to do that for the first time in a scalable way."

Despite the mounting evidence that today's sharing economy has drastically shifted customer expectations, many corporations still don't get it. They view customer service as just another cost center. But unless they recognize that today, reputation is *everything,* these companies will not survive.

This leaves a huge window of opportunity open for you, a leader who creates change from the inside out. Your job is to not only make your service remarkable, but take it out of the public relations realm and weave it into the fabric of everything your company does by continually asking yourself:

- Are we living and breathing our mission and core values?
- Are we proud of how we serve our customers—both externally and internally?

- Are our customers noticing how we serve them?
- Are we asking our customers to tell people about their great experiences with us in the form of referrals, testimonials, case studies, and online reviews?

Customer happiness should be your top priority. Empower your team to deliver highly responsive, bend-over-backwards, high-quality support both in person and online. Show customers that you genuinely care about the issues they are facing (and fix them quickly).

As we discussed in Chapter 6, chances are that other companies are providing the same basic products and services as you. That's not what makes you unique. Or at least—it won't be for very long. What differentiates your company is your Remarkable Selling Point, your service delivery, and your people.

In this chapter, we're going to go a step further. We're going to talk about how to use what's special about your company—your Remarkable Selling Point—to turn your prospects not only into customers, but *engaged customers.* People who don't just use your product, but who talk about it. People who don't just write you a check for your services, but loyal customers who are keenly aware of the value you bring them and see you as a true strategic partner.

Exceed expectations, always in all ways

Engaging your customers means going above and beyond good service and actually exceeding their expectations. Often it can be the little ongoing gestures that make the big differences—and these don't have to cost a lot of money.

The Portland-based virtual receptionists company, Ruby Receptionists, cares so much about delighting its customers that one of its core values is "Practice Wowism." As Ruby Receptionists says, "We're not just about answering phones. We're about finding that special something that will knock your socks off, and giving it to you before you even know you want it."

Ruby Receptionists is so dedicated to making meaningful connections—internally and externally—that its employees are measured based on how well they cultivate relationships with callers, clients, and other colleagues, says CEO Jill Nelson. Ruby encourages its employees to practice random acts of kindness by using its prepaid Amazon account and a "WOW station" stocked with gifts and cards to surprise coworkers and clients at any time.

"We're about making people happy here at Ruby, and to achieve this, it starts internally with our staff," says Nelson. "We invest heavily in employee leadership programs, create community-building opportunities, and develop initiatives that cultivate happiness inside and out."

In other words, they start from the inside.

This relentless dedication to customer service (to both external and internal customers) catapulted Ruby's growth year over year from $3.9 million in 2010 to more than $20 million in 2016.

When you build this kind of customer service-centric organization from the inside out, customers will want to find every excuse to do more business with you. According to a recent survey by American Express, more than two thirds of American consumers say they're willing to spend 14 percent more on average with a company that they believe delivers excellent service. And virtually all respondents in that same study said that being connected to someone knowledgeable (98 percent) is an important prerequisite to a great customer experience.[52]

Remember, you want repeat customers. According to Frederick Reichheld of Bain & Company, just a 5 percent increase in customer retention can increase business profits by anywhere between 25 percent and 85 percent. Returning customers spend more money with you in subsequent transactions. As they do, your operating costs to service them go down. And they will often be willing to pay a pre-mium to continue to do business with your company rather than switch to one of your competitors with whom they do not have an established relationship.[53]

There is a direct correlation between a work environment that advocates for its customers and one with engaged, positive employ-ees.[54] Many studies have shown that when your team members are happy and engaged, they go the extra mile, resulting in positive orga-nizational performance outcomes including employee retention, productivity, profitability, customer loyalty, and safety.[55]

Remember United and their long-standing reputation for poor customer service?

Contrast this with JetBlue Airways. According to researchers at the well-known management firm Bain & Company, the key ingre-dient to JetBlue's success is that their employees are encouraged to treat customers' problems as if they are their own.

"Running late for a flight? You might be escorted by a JetBlue counter agent to an employees-only security line, right through to the gate. Putting together a complicated multi-stop trip? The call center agent will work with you to arrive at a satisfactory solution, not rush you off the phone. JetBlue staff members focus intensely on making the customers' lives easier, and customers repay the courtesy by spreading the word to others."

JetBlue works hard to take care of its employees, knowing that their positive behavior and attitude will translate to their customers, igniting their passion, loyalty, and referrals.[56]

Forbes columnist Ben Kepes flies well over a quarter of a million miles a year. To say he knows airlines would be an understatement. He lives in New Zealand so his typical airline is Air New Zealand and Star Alliance partner United. He had the occasion to take a JetBlue flight in 2015 so—as is his habit—he tweeted, "This morning I'm flying @JetBlue for the first time in my life. Amazin [sic] consider I do well over a quarter million miles a year."

Within seconds, JetBlue responded with this Tweet:

"We can't wait to have you onboard, Ben! Where are you off to today?"

There was then an exchange of Tweets with JetBlue telling Ben that there was a "nice surprise waiting for him at check-in." It turns out that JetBlue had bumped Ben up to first class.

Ben was so impressed he wrote a column about the experience and tweeted it to his more than twenty thousand followers.

Whomever the engaged employees were that took good care of Ben on Twitter and in his upgrade did an amazing job at creating a brilliant customer experience that resulted in free public relations.

Nobody raves about average

So how do you start creating a culture that focuses on customer engagement? We have good news—you've already started the process by crafting your One-Word Mission™, Big Vision, and Living, Breathing Values™. In a corporate executive board study published by the *Harvard Business Review*, of the consumers who said they have a brand relationship, 64 percent cited shared the company's values as the primary reason.[57]

By focusing on and over-communicating what's important to you, you ensure your employees are treating one another and your customers with respect and integrity. You also draw in those customers who align with your values and mission, which is an important factor many leaders overlook. Before we dive deeper, here are a few simple strategies for building a culture of engagement:

- Take a close look at your processes and systems for interacting with your customers. Are they fostering a human touch and emotional connection? Or have you put a barrier of technology in place that does nothing but frustrate your customers (i.e., long on-hold times, complicated automated phone trees, complex forms, etc.)?

- Next look at your people. Are you training them to treat prospects with respect, patience, and attentiveness? Do they communicate with your customers in a fashion that is clear, professional, and kind? Are they consistently delivering on your Remarkable Selling Point (RSP)?

As a small- to mid-sized business, you have a huge advantage over the big corporations—you can provide a level of service they cannot. As just a few examples, your company can:

- have your CEO call your customers to check in to see how they are doing. This makes a huge impression.
- ask managers to observe and listen to the customer experience directly to look for improvements.
- encourage account representatives to know your customers well so they can make specific recommendations that are custom to their unique needs.
- quickly move to solve problems and change the customer experience when you discover a process isn't working.
- develop deep relationships with your customers and take a consultant-like approach to help them make the best decisions related to your area of expertise.
- respond to customers' evolving needs rapidly by developing new service and product lines as soon as they show a demand.

Take advantage of this opportunity to shine and actually get in front of your customers' needs. Research shows that 70 percent of buying experiences are based on how your customers feel about the way they are being treated.[58] Hire people who are in alignment with your commitment to customer advocacy. And then from the moment they come onboard, emphasize to your employees that they—like JetBlue—should treat customers' problems as their own.

Let's take a look at the history of JetBlue to see how they grew their passionate commitment to both their employees and their customers.

In 1984, along with June Morris, David Neeleman cofounded his first business, Morris Air, a low-fare charter airline, which was eventually acquired by Southwest Airlines. A consummate entrepreneur, Neeleman went on to cofound WestJet (a Canadian regional airline) and develop Open Skies (an electronic ticketing system).

In 1998, he founded New Air Corporation which changed its name to JetBlue the following year. The name of the company was different, but Neeleman was committed to his original idea of low-cost air flight and exceptional service. Their Big Vision? "Become the Americas' favorite airline by bringing humanity back to air travel."

Long-term success meant delivering magnificent service during every flight and in every interaction. Passengers enjoyed free cobranded amenities such as brand-name snacks, Dunkin' Donuts coffee, XM satellite radio, DIRECTV satellite television, and Bliss Spa comfort kits. In flight, people could watch live TV, purchase inflight movies, and sip wine from local New York shops. The company also innovated to please its customers—from inception, JetBlue has had ticketless travel, one-way fares, and assigned seats.

And while the company has had some ups and downs, they are one of the few recent successful start-ups in the competitive U.S. airline business. They have weathered tremendous economic pressures, including those influenced by the changes wrought by September 11, rising fuel costs in the early 2000s, and heavy industry debt loads. In spite of these challenges, Jet Blue has remained committed to its vision and the happiness of both its employees and its customers.

It has been awarded "Top Low Cost Airline for Customer Satisfaction" by J.D. Power and Associates eleven years in a row, and in 2015 ranked #19 in *Forbes* magazine's "America's Top 500 Best Employers."

"You have to remain focused on your people," said Neeleman. "That's the key to great service."

JetBlue's commitment to service worked for B2C. But how do we translate their techniques for a B2B market? B2B buyers tend to have much larger budgets, longer buying cycles, and repeat purchases. They also have much higher expectations when it comes to customer service. And when you lose a client, it represents thousands, hundreds of thousands—or even millions—in revenue for your company.

That's why, as a B2B organization, it's perhaps even more imperative for your operational practices to be in alignment with your mission, values, and RSP. It's crucial that you deliver on your brand promise each and every time. In the best B2B relationships, the supplier intimately knows the client's business and industry. These high-performing B2B companies develop great relationships with key stakeholders, and they take a long-term view of the association. They are continuously on the lookout for win-win scenarios—meaning, they bring new ideas for customer engagement.

Gallup research has put numbers to the power of customer engagement: customers who are fully engaged enjoy an average 23 percent premium in terms of wallet share, profitability, revenue, and relationship growth compared with the average customer across industries. Companies that engage both their employees and their customers gain a mind-blowing 240 percent boost in performance-related business outcomes compared to companies that don't focus on those activities. That's some compelling evidence.[59]

CUSTOMER ENGAGEMENT IS A JOURNEY

EVERY CUSTOMER INTERACTION MATTERS—FROM THEIR first glance at your website to the call they place with the receptionist to your delivery of the final product. Let's explore some ways you can easily improve your customers' experiences at every touchpoint.

1. **First impressions count:** You know the saying "Never judge a book by its cover"? It may be a robust life philosophy, but it definitely doesn't apply to online consumer behavior.

   Snap judgments are a fact of life in the world of B2B decision-making. Did you know that it takes no more than fifty milliseconds[60] (that's 0.05 seconds) for users to form an opinion about your website? That's all a user needs to determine whether they like your site or not, whether they'll stay or leave. If they don't like it—CLICK!—off to another site.

   Great web design instills trust in your business. According to research from Stanford, 75 percent of users admit to making judgments about a company's credibility based on their website's design.[61] In a day and age where 85 percent of B2B customers search the web before making a purchase decision,[62] your website is likely your prospect's "first impression" of your company and offerings. And—here's what really might surprise you—more than half of all B2B researchers are Millennials.[63]

Your website is your opportunity to begin your relationship with a "Wow!"—before prospects even become customers. Interestingly, positive first impressions can prime their perception of future interactions with your business. Research shows that positive priming can boost user satisfaction and, as you might expect, negative first impressions put significant drag on user satisfaction.[64]

This priming effect can last years. And it applies to all of human psychology. One study found that the NBA players' careers are determined by their position in the draft, regardless of their on-court performance.[65] Another found that subsequent impressions, no matter how contradictory, can never make up for the first impression—bringing a literal meaning to the saying that "you never get a second chance to make a first impression."[66]

So in your online marketing, always remember that today's internet user has infinite sites vying for their attention. In a crowded, competitive landscape, it's crucial to carve out a space where your brand and your offerings stand out, grab, and hold the attention of your dream customers. In just a few minutes, your potential customers will form an opinion about your company and your competitors:

- Is this company up-to-date with trends?
- Are they professional and organized?
- Does this organization have credible case studies and testimonials from other businesses like mine?
- Do they have experience in my industry?
- What are their areas of expertise and specific skill-sets?
- Can they solve my precise problem?
- What is the background of their leadership team?

- How is their approach unique?
- Are their mission and values in alignment with ours?

Potential customers will drill down into the content on your website, so make sure to showcase your knowledge and convince your dream customers you have the right solutions to their specific problem.

2. **Your online reputation is far-reaching:** B2B buyers—like B2C buyers—will do extensive research before making a purchase. And you can bet they'll turn to online reviews. A recent study of more than fourteen hundred B2B customers found that they had completed, on average, more than 60 percent of their purchasing decision *before* ever having a conversation with a supplier.[67]

   And they won't stop there. Prospects will also go to your company page on LinkedIn and review your team members' experiences and endorsements.

   Many of our B2B clients have been surprised to discover negative reviews of their company on places like Google and Yelp. And—be aware—the rising popularity of sites like Glassdoor give your disgruntled employees and potential hires (yup, the bad-fit candidates you never wanted) ample opportunities to review your company.

   But this isn't bad news. If you are proactive, you can encourage your customers (both external and internal) to give you honest reviews online. And—if you are providing exceptional service—most of them will not only be happy to do so, but will leave glowing reviews. While it is almost impossible to have negative reviews removed, you can always ask your former customer or employee how you can resolve the issue—and, once you have, politely inquire as to whether they'd consider changing or removing their review. Your second option is to write an honest response to the criticism.

After you've assessed your online presence, take the steps to put a system in place to regularly ask for reviews. When doing so:

- tell customers and employees you are looking for their honest feedback.
- empower your entire team to ask for reviews. Everyone at your company is an ambassador and should make a request when the moment arises.
- ask customers through multiple channels—on your website, on the phone, on social media, in meetings, and so on.
- make it easy for customers to give you reviews by providing them instructions (for example, not everyone will know how to leave a Google review).
- thank customers and employees for giving their feedback.
- work to get a good number of reviews. An ample amount of online reviews is powerful in helping a potential customer or employee choose your organization.

3. **You should map your sales process:** Too many companies leave their sales process up to the whims of their sales teams—and it's a mistake. The sales process is your prospects' earliest experience with your brand and—as such—should be carefully managed. Because, remember, those first impressions matter.

We recommend you create a sales process that is systematized, with established milestones that mark the key events as your prospects move along the sales cycle. Create a sales map that shows your sales team the blow-by-blow process that they should be taking in order to convert your inquiries into customers. This can include steps for building trust, under-standing your buyers' goals, creating certainty that your offers meet their needs, and so on. Be open to letting your process evolve over time.

Once your salespeople qualify a prospect as a dream cus-tomer, carefully define the follow-up action they should take. As customers move deeper in your sales pipeline, how do your sales people educate them about the breadth of your services and let them know what's to come?

Once a lead expresses interest about your specific offerings, it's important that your company has a set way to present your organization. This may be an in-person meeting, an online sales demo, a white paper you send out, or a presentation you give to them. This is your opportunity to showcase your company's differences and start adding value to the relationship. Yes, your salespeople won't want to plan everything—give them a little room to practice the "art of selling"—but look for opportunities to standardize the process throughout the organization. We recom-mend that this includes diligent notes in a customer relationship management (CRM) system so leadership can track activities and generate reports. Then make sure your sales process is being fol-lowed. Train your new salespeople on the process and hold your existing salespeople accountable for demonstrating that they are following your new sales process map. You may want to include feedback in your regular sales huddles and incorporate specific requirements that you set in your sales teams' goal setting and review in your annual performance meeting.

4. **Create a customer onboarding system:** The sales process doesn't end when your prospect says, "Yes, I'll buy." We recommend a standard onboarding system that delivers an incredible welcome

and starts adding value right away. Lack of follow-up can cause customers to have buyer's regret. And a hard handoff from sales to customer service with no transition can create a jarring experience.

Consider a planned orientation process for each new client where you warmly welcome them and teach them how to get the most from what they've agreed to buy. A smooth transition from prospect to customer (and sales person to account manager) sets the tone for additional purchases and referrals. You could wrap in many resources for onboarding including a welcome packet, email, phone call, visit, gift, handwritten thank you card, and/ or videos. Examples of information you could provide to them includes: a message from your CEO and/or account representative, an explanation of how they can get the most out of your services, an introduction to the team members who will be serving them, documentation on how to use any software or systems you have, an explanation of what is coming next for your customer, and an invitation to ask any questions they have and an offer of assistance. Your number one goal is to increase their engagement right away and showcase your remarkability. Keep them feeling like they just made the best decision in the world by hiring your company (because they did, right?).

The excitement your client felt during the sales process is still fresh. You can capitalize on it and get your new customer committed to packages and projects (remember those productized services?). Jump into the work quickly so that you can show value and ROI right away. The earlier you can show success, the better your ongoing relationship with your client will be. A solid foundation of results in the initial planning phase of your Service Delivery Map makes it easy to up-sell the client after the ramp-up/assessment phase.

Now we recognize that every service-centric company will have slightly different parameters for their kickoff, but the same general format that we outline below can serve as a model for most B2B companies:

- Send an email or call your new customer within a day of the contract being signed. This email should be focused on thanking them for their business, explaining the initial scope of work, introducing team members and outlining their roles and responsibilities, sharing contact information, and requesting dates/times of your initial kickoff meeting.

- We also recommend sending out a new client questionnaire that not only provides you with helpful information that will save time during the kickoff meeting, but that also provides value to your client by helping them think through their issues more deeply and thoughtfully. Include the agenda and purpose for your kickoff meeting.

- Your kickoff meeting should include all stakeholders within the company. The goal is a deeper connection—you want to make sure your team and key stakeholders of the client's team are on the same page. You should reaffirm goals and agreed-upon solutions that were discussed in the sales process. By asking the right questions, outlining the scope of work, and setting expectations for the work, your relationship is set up for success. One caveat for this kickoff meeting: since you will have higher-level decision-makers attending, make sure you keep the discussion from getting into the nitty-gritty details. This is a waste of their time and a missed opportunity for you to create bonds.

- Afterward send out the notes from the meeting that include any specific deliverables, descriptions, timelines, budgets, and individuals responsible. Set up your meeting rhythms moving forward, both with the frontline team members that will be working on the tactical components, as well as the high-level meetings where you will update decision-makers on progress and results.

5. **Every touchpoint matters:** Now consider the rest of your customers' journey. What is their experience at each touchpoint? Many B2B companies fail to pay attention to the customer's entire journey.

    Remember: every time your customers are interacting with your brand, they are becoming either more engaged or less engaged. You increase your clients' engagement by ensuring that each touch provides a consistent message and high level of service. Wow! them at every turn.

    Most likely, your clients are receiving numerous email and phone exchanges with various representatives from your organization. Some questions to consider:

    - Is each team member working to Wow! your client when it's their turn to encounter your customer? Not just the account representative—what about your receptionist and your billing department?
    - What about when your customer is at a meeting and uses the restroom? Is it tidy and does it have extras?
    - Are you providing nice drinks and snacks at your meetings?
    - Do your people respond to inquiries within a day?
    - Is your waiting area comfortable with interesting reading material?

- When your customers come to your office or facility, can they see your employees' desks or workspaces? If so, are these kept tidy and professional?
- When someone comes in to your office or facility, are they greeted immediately (even if you don't have a dedicated front receptionist)?
- Do you have a confusing or irritating automated phone tree that your customers have to navigate when they call? How long are they kept on hold?

While they may only account for a small percentage of actual time spent interacting with your customer, each piece of the puzzle shapes your customers' brand experience. Carefully examine *all* the ways your team interacts with your customers and determine how you can optimize each and every touchpoint. Even the smallest detail can have an impact.

As you move your client through your Service Delivery Map (the overarching set of steps that your customer goes through as they engage with your company), make sure that you are producing tangible, positive, and meaningful results for your customers. Reinforce that you are there in partnership with them to solve their problems and meet their needs. Within your culture, continuously reinforce the need to be customer-centric—your team is on an ongoing mission to impress your entire client organization.

BACK TO YOUR EMPLOYEES

"Clients do not come first. Employees come first.
If you take care of your employees, they will
take care of your clients."

—Richard Branson

THE FOCUS OF THIS CHAPTER HAS BEEN ON CUSTOMER engagement, but don't forget that engaged employees are incredibly important to the health and vigor of your company. And that engaged employees result in engaged customers.

Engaged employees go the extra mile for your customers. They strive to build and nurture long-term customer relationships. Armed with a deep connection to the company's mission, values, and vision, and with reinforcement from leadership, engaged staff focus on optimizing every customer interaction, create emotional connections with customers, and work to stay ahead of their customers' needs—at every touchpoint.

Authentic customer engagement is born from a culture that believes that clients should be acknowledged, helped, thanked, and recognized for their loyalty. Basically everyone in your company should be invested in keeping your customers happy. Let's look at some specific systems you can put into place in your organization to encourage and motivate your team to Wow! your customers.

The remarkable power of gratitude and recognition

Gratitude and recognition are simple, yet powerful. An easy thing to forget in the midst of our frenzied work lives is the simple act of saying "thank you" and recognizing people for their accomplishments.

Who has the time to slow down for such old-fashioned pleasantries? And yet, by incorporating this into your marketing efforts, your company will reap immense rewards.

You'll actually stand out from your competitors because it is typically not something that other businesses are in the habit of doing. Sadly (but luckily for you), extending age-old courtesies now actually gives you an edge in the marketplace. It's become a lost art. And it goes a long way toward both cementing relationships with prospects and reinforcing customer loyalty. Your customers want to feel valued and that your relationship with them matters.

One of the most personal ways to thank or recognize someone is a handwritten card. Encourage your sales team, your account executives, and your leadership team to get into the habit of writing notes. Have them keep a stack by their desk and scribble notes to customers and prospects. Once your company gets in the habit of writing notes, your team will find limitless opportunities. And guess what? People are tickled pink to receive a good, old-fashioned card.

Make sure that leadership reinforces that notes should be sincere messages, not thinly-disguised sales pitches. People like to feel appreciated and recognized. So you can write notes of congratulations when your customers (and prospects) win an award, when they get press, when they launch a new website, when they introduce a new product/service, when they move into a new building, and so on.

You can also acknowledge them when they first become a customer, when they celebrate an anniversary of working with your company, when they pass other milestones at your business, when they refer someone to you, when they give you feedback, when they sign up for a new service, when they say something nice about your company or employees, when they come to your facility for a meeting, when it's a holiday, and so on.

Customer retention program

As we mentioned, the B2B realm has been slower to realize that their customers are taking greater control by seeking information and opinions to shape their purchase and renewal decisions. B2B organizations continue to spend most of their marketing budget on lead acquisition, brand-building, and filling the pipeline—and yet they have a lot to gain by creating a customer-obsessed culture that focuses all team members on loyalty.

One of the easiest ways to support your culture in its efforts is a customer-appreciation program. When thinking about how to structure it, start with your end goal in mind: what behaviors do you want to influence as a result of your efforts? Then, establish metrics and specific goals.

We recommend starting your program with the top 20 percent of your customers. Go back to the Principle 5 of the book on dream clients and look at the 5-Star Client exercise. If you'll recall, the "A" category represents the clients who are spending the most money with your company and who are the most profitable, strategic, and the most likely to be loyal. By starting your customer appreciation efforts with them, your organization will see the biggest impact on your revenue, profits, and retention metrics.

Evaluate how well you are managing your relationships with these A-level clients:

- Are you communicating with them regularly?
- Are you approaching them from an account-based perspective—in other words, is there a person in your organization who meets with each client regularly and drives communications and deepens connections?
- Are you monitoring the news and social media for mentions of these clients (and then showing them that you noticed)?

- Is your team working together—across functions—to serve and delight each of these A-level clients?

Next take a look at the ways in which you reward your A-level clients. Become a generous brand that recognizes your customers for their purchases and accomplishments, and adds ongoing value. Then once you get your customer-appreciation methods dialed in with your A-level clients, you can extend efforts throughout all of your accounts.

Here are some specific suggestions for B2B companies looking to build a customer-obsessed culture:

1. **Ensure your employees have the right resources:** The individuals who are on the front line of delivering your customer experience need tools and authority to solve customers' problems. Make sure you are always informing, educating, and coaching your employees to excel at interactions with your customers.

2. **Be prepared for resistance:** Be forewarned: when you first set this system in motion you are likely to get pushback. "But we already do this. We provide great service!" Accepting the notion that it could be better still can be a hard pill to swallow for your employees so be ready to address resistance head-on. Align your team with your One-Word Mission™ and Living, Breathing Values™, and then help them see that improving customer engagement is a journey. There is no *there* to get to, because you are on a quest to continuously strive for the next level of excellence.

3. **Recognize your clients for reaching milestones and achievements:** First, make sure that your team is empowered to spend a pre-allocated amount on small gifts for your clients. When you

learn of something that your client company has accomplished (either because they tell you or you see it in the news or on social media), send a card and a gift saying "Congratulations!" Make the gift elegant and meaningful (it doesn't have to be expensive, just thoughtful). You can also take your client out to lunch, dinner, a drink, coffee, or an event to celebrate. This bonding is a fantastic way to deepen your relationships with key customers. You can also add a congratulations on social media. Remember, even in the B2B space, your clients are people and everyone likes to be recognized.

4. **Make sure you are building relationships with decision-makers:** In the best B2B retention efforts, your dedicated account manager is building and nurturing relationships with the senior executives, as well as the mid-level managers. The top leaders must be aware of the value your company is bringing to them on a regular basis—they are the ones with the real purchasing power. You may interact with a business client that has a buying center, with multiple people responsible for committing their dollars to a particular solution or partner. If this is the case, ensure your relationship managers build connections with as many stakeholders as possible. Establishing regular meeting rhythms and delivering progress reports is helpful in this endeavor.

5. **Give customers new ideas and continuously add value:** Approach relationships from a consultative perspective. During your client meetings, focus on how you can add value to your customers, always striving to provide meaningful impact to their company. This could involve increasing efficiencies, saving money, enhancing your clients' standing in the marketplace, improving their supply chain management, augmenting their processes,

and so on. An advice-based approach deepens customer relationships. It provides a "stickiness" that is difficult to duplicate because your competitors don't have the same access to knowledge that you have. It's one more way to fortify your curtain wall, keeping your customers "cozy and warm inside your castle." If you don't currently have this structure in place, it can be a difficult shift to make. You may have account managers who tell you "that's not part of my job" or "I don't have the time to do that!" From their perspective, their responsibility is to sell and service the account—not to improve their customers' bottom line.

If this is the case in your company, let your relationship managers know that working to add impact to their accounts doesn't negate the impact of quality, service, responsiveness, etc. Instead, help them to see that these are all things your competitors can do too. Show them that creating true partnerships with your customers will set you apart from competitors, uphold your mission and values, strengthen your curtain wall, and result in long-term account growth and revenues.

To create real impact for your customers (and enhance retention), they must continue to satisfy all of the functional requirements *and* produce positive, lucrative impacts for your clients with high levels of emotional engagement. (A word of caution: some of your old-school team members may not be able to make the shift with you.)

6. **Regularly talk with your clients about their business goals:** Develop a system wherein your relationship managers habitually ask your customers about their business goals. Have your leadership team work to create business-level plans to help meet your clients' goals and solve their problems. Build in team member accountability and list specific performance metrics for success.

Don't forget to ask your customers where they are headed. Explore the opportunities for new offerings with them: are there services/products that your company could develop for them that would help them achieve their goals? What can you help them with to go further?

7. **Know your next steps:** When you are done helping them with your current solution, what is the next step for your clients? In chapter 6, we described how to create your Service Delivery Map—when you reach your last step (as a reminder, this is typically a measurement or evaluation), how can you circle back around to your Step 1 research phase and initiate the next service? Always ask yourself: how can I help my client achieve more?

8. **Set appropriate performance goals and measure outcomes:** Set specific performance goals for your team members that support your overall organizational goals. Ensure you are moving away from goals such as "average call time" that only measure quantity—and instead set up metrics that actually gauge the customer experience (i.e., customer satisfaction, Net Promoter score, loyalty, referral rates, etc.). Link performance rewards directly to the quality of the customer experience.

Remember, engaged employees are the lifeblood of your organization. Their passion in your mission, values, and vision are what will create a remarkable customer experience. Engaged employees go the extra mile for your customers, building and nurturing these relationships. From sales to purchase to engagement to retention, B2B companies have everything to gain from building a customer-obsessed culture. Often this requires substantial changes in culture and mind-set, but it pays off with superior growth of both top- and bottom-line revenue.

Working from the inside out to heighten both employee and customer engagement has the added benefit of positively changing people's lives—your organization becomes one where your team loves to come to work. They are happy, motivated, and find a deeper sense of purpose every day. They feel heard and supported, and—as a result—they make every effort to please your customers. Your customers love working with you and get incredible value. By creating this type of company, you are impacting many lives in a positive way. Plus it creates a pretty great place for you to work too!

PRINCIPLE #10

GROWTH REQUIRES BOTH STRATEGIC PLANNING AND EXECUTION

"Good business leaders create a vision,
articulate the vision, passionately own the vision,
and relentlessly drive it to completion."

—Jack Welch, former CEO of General Electric

BY NOW, YOU HAVE EVERYTHING YOU NEED TO GROW YOUR business from the inside out. However, if these strategies aren't systematically implemented into your organization and operationalized, then you've just wasted your valuable time reading these chapters. Our goal for you is to weave the new practices and ideas you've developed into the fabric of your business.

This requires planning.

Unfortunately, most strategic planning fails. In a *McKinsey Quarterly* survey of nearly 800 executives, just 45 percent said they were satisfied with their strategic planning process. What's worse, only 23 percent indicated that major strategic decisions were made during this process.[68]

Many companies we've worked have told us similar stories about their disastrous attempts at implementing new systems in their companies. After spending days or even weeks in thrilling brainstorming mode, there was usually a true sense of enthusiasm about the work they did together. But these teams never created a systematic process for moving toward their goals. They didn't hold specific people responsible for getting actions completed nor did they create a system for checking in on goal progress.

As a result, all those great ideas were stashed away on a metaphorical shelf to gather metaphorical dust.

If this describes a scenario that has happened at your organization, you aren't alone. In fact, you are in very good company. We find it's very common for companies to underestimate the work it takes to systematize new processes and practices.

Not only is it a huge waste of leadership's time, energy, and money to expend efforts learning a methodology they never implement, it's frustrating and demoralizing for everyone. When employees hear about leadership dabbling in another system or philosophy that has no real impact on the company, it creates feelings of doubt and uncertainty.

Here's how one dispirited executive described the planning process: "No one is exactly sure why we do it, but there is an almost mystical hope that something good will come out of it."[69]

He's right about one thing: something good should come out of it! But it's up to you as the leader to ensure that something does.

THE TEN REASONS WHY MOST STRATEGIC PLANNING FAILS

ONE OF OUR CLIENTS—AN ENGINEERING AND CONSTRUCTION firm called Blakeland Group—are led by a husband and wife team who have lots of on-the-fly, big dream, where-we-are-going types of conversations while driving or making dinner.

What they lacked, however, was a formal process for setting a Big Vision, then breaking it down into smaller goals and steps. As a result, the company was doing well enough, but it wasn't achieving the level of remarkability that Marcus and Katie knew they could achieve.

If your planning process looks anything like Blakeland Group's—and many of our other clients—it's either sporadic, nonexistent, or inefficient. In our experience, most companies fall into one of the following categories:

1. **There is no formal process:** Many organizations do not have annual or semi-annual strategic planning—or they may only have ad-hoc meetings with no real rhythm.

2. **Attendees lack adequate preparation:** If no one preps for the planning sessions, decisions are made without inadequate information.

3. **Sessions are data dumps with no discussions about vision:** Planning is focused on operational and financial projections but there is no discussion about the larger strategic issues that could impact the company, nor are people looking out into the future at opportunities and threats.

4. **Meetings are all ideas, no real plan:** It's common for people to spend the majority of their strategic planning sessions brainstorming ideas and having passionate discussions. And we get it: it feels good to be in creation mode. Oh just think of the things you'll do! But without proper plans for implementation, the ideas will languish in a file folder when your people return to their day-to-day efforts.

5. **Meetings lack a clearly defined agenda:** No one puts together an agenda, so participants are not productive or timely. As a result, the day becomes an extended, ineffective meeting.

6. **Key decision-makers are missing:** When key stakeholders are missing, not only is it hard to make good decisions during your planning session, but you risk post-meeting idea sabotage and work scope creep when those who were absent start weighing in after the fact.

7. **Strategy is not communicated:** Even if a planning session is productive, if leadership does a poor job of communicating the strategy throughout the organization, there will be little buy-in from individuals and departments tasked with implementation.

8. **There is no actionable follow-up:** If big goals are not broken down into bite-sized chunks and assigned to the proper departments or leadership does not allocate time and other resources necessary, a strategic initiative is set up for failure.

9. **There's no accountability:** Too many companies fail to assign individuals to lead initiatives, or set up dates, timelines, and follow-up meetings.

10. **Lack of flexibility:** Of all of the barricades to successful implementation, this might be our biggest pet peeve. Even if your team addresses all the previous challenges and roadblocks, your strategic plans will still fall short if they aren't developed with flexibility.

Now that we've touched upon some of the reasons strategic initiatives fail, we're going to talk about how to do it right.

SUCCESSFUL STRATEGIC PLANNING AND EXECUTION

"The greatest strategy is doomed if it's implemented badly."

—Bernard Reimann

WE VIEW STRATEGIC PLANNING AS A DISCIPLINED EFFORT. It requires setting priorities for your company, focusing your resources on specific efforts, and ensuring your team members are moving toward common goals—ideally, both the executive team's financial goals as well as your organization's Big Vision.

The Marketing From the Inside Out® approach only works when leaders put new systems in place that support these ideas and techniques. But it's not just our methodology that requires this deep level of support and direction from top leadership—in our experience, it's a must-have when it comes to introducing any new company-wide process or strategy. Without plans for execution, new ideas and strategies do nothing but get people excited for a very short time.

Since we can't take you all through the strategic planning process personally, this chapter presents a basic framework for implementation and accountability.

This process has worked for leaders who are ready to start rolling out the Marketing From the Inside Out® method—but we've found these four steps are equally effective when it comes to introducing any major initiative throughout the organization.

STEP ONE. *Prepare for your first strategic planning session*

When we work with our clients, we always start with an initial strategic planning session with the company's leadership team. This session has two major goals:

1. First, it is an opportunity to develop a plan for sharing and operationalizing the ideas you've come up with after reading this book. By now, you should have identified your mission, vision, and values (to name just a few things) and in this session, you're going to think about new systems to help your employees live and breathe your company's most important beliefs and aspirations.

2. Second, it is the time to discuss all your specific goals, activities, and timelines which you'll be establishing over the next six to twelve months.

We've learned that these sessions are much more effective when there's a fair bit of planning before the meeting itself. Here are the steps we recommend.

1. **Decide the date and location for the meeting:** We recommend getting out of the office so you don't have any interruptions.

2. **Decide who should attend:** Unless you have managers who are very accustomed to thinking strategically and planning at the highest level of your company, we recommend only your top leadership be involved. This may mean only the owners/partners—or perhaps it also includes some or all of your executives. Use your discretion and consider the size of your organization as well as the level of sophistication in your leaders.

3. **Pull together any documents that will help describe the current state of your business—and your goals for the future:** Asking the following question prior to the session itself will help you hit the ground running:

   How would you describe your current situation (financial, culture, marketing, sales, positioning, service delivery, customer engagement and retention, hiring and performance, etc.)?

4. **Plan to discuss the rollout of your Marketing From the Inside Out® strategy:** Make sure you've made decisions about the foundational aspects of the Marketing From the Inside Out® method prior to your first annual strategic planning session. This will help you plan more effectively across all aspects of your company:

   - Living, Breathing Values™ (LBVs)
   - One-Word Mission™
   - Big Vision
   - Remarkable Selling Point (RSP)
   - Your dream clients and their pain points

If you haven't done this work yet, then we strongly recommend you go back to the previous chapters before setting up your planning session. The following questions will help you plan your rollout activities:

- Can your entire staff clearly communicate our organization's mission, values, and Big Vision? If not, please describe the gaps.
- Are there things that you will need to roll out in your company to shift your culture to align with each aspect of your Marketing From the Inside Out® strategy?
- What should happen over the next six to twelve months to improve your culture?

5. **Feel free to add other questions to the mix:** The point is to get you and the rest of the leadership team thinking big picture. It may take your team a while to answer these questions—especially if you've never thought about them. But be sure to set a deadline—and hold team members accountable for completing them prior to your strategic planning session.

Additional prep work may include gathering performance data from your company and relevant departments. Here are some of the things that our clients come prepared to discuss:

- Revenue
- Revenue streams from discrete service areas (revenue centers)
- Net profit
- Average customer tenure
- Average spend per customer (customer lifetime value)
- Customer acquisition cost

- Debt load
- Marketing budget
- Success metrics (these vary greatly from company to company)

You may only have some of this information—and that's okay. Many of our clients have never set an annual marketing budget or dissected each customer's lifetime value. Put together what you have right now—that will form the foundation for your strategic planning sessions.

6. **Set a rhythm for these big strategic planning sessions:** In order to succeed, your strategic planning sessions need to have their own six-month rhythms: these are regular, consistent planning sessions that your leaders commit to attending. It will start with your first one, which will be one to two full days. Your first one should focus on the roll out of the items listed in Item 4 above.

   After that, plan for and commit to having an annual and a semi-annual strategic planning session every six months. The semi-annual meetings typically last four to six hours, and the annual lasts a full day. Ideally you can time these so they coincide with the calendar year, although that isn't essential.

   As you begin to set up implementation meeting rhythms (more about that in a moment) and reap the rewards of executing your strategy, you can become increasingly sophisticated in the data you collect. Perhaps developing some additional metrics will be one of your strategic planning initiatives.

STEP TWO: Create a blueprint for the next six to twelve months during your strategic planning session.

Your major goal during this one- to two-day session is to create a blueprint for *only* the next six to twelve months. The action steps your leadership team commits to in each strategic planning session are the stepping stones that will help your company reach its one-year goal, three- to five-year goals, and, ultimately move you closer to realizing your Big Vision.

1. **Determine the "State of the Business":** Now is the time to leverage the prep work you did prior to the strategic planning session, especially your metrics. First, take a look at where you are now (sales data, cash flow, growth, budgets, and so on). We call this the "State of the Business."

2. **Set your three- to five-year goals:** While you're going to be creating a blueprint for *only* the next six to twelve months, start your session by setting your three- to five-year goals. These are the mile markers along the path that you must accomplish in order for your business to achieve your Big Vision. Unlike your Big Vision, these goals are more practical and less aspirational. It's crucial to lay down these stepping stones because they will accelerate your progress toward your ultimate outcome.

    Be sure to set a realistic number of goals. Many of our clients pick three or four. You want to set your company up for success, so do not pick any goals that seem unattainable. Here are some ideas:

    - Increase our revenue to X
    - Purchase a building
    - Enter new geographic markets
    - Launch specific service/product lines

- Increase number of employees to X (or by X percent)
- Reduce staff turnover by X percent
- Increase customer lifetime value by X

3. **Identify your six- to twelve-month goals:** Once you have your three- to five-year goals, your next objective is to back into your six- to twelve-month goals. What necessary steps does your company need to take to reach your five-year goals? These should be easy to determine since they are really just benchmarks along the way. Each goal builds upon the next.

    Remember the company RedBalloon that we discussed in Chapter 4? You may recall the company's leaders set a Big Vision of *providing 10 percent of Australia's twenty million citizens with a gifted experience.*

    Because their Big Vision was so, well, *big* they needed to put into place stepping stones along the way—targets around their sales, social media outreach, geographic locations, web presence, and technology, for example. The company also had to ensure they had the right people on board—managers, sales team, and customer service representatives—who could meet these targets.

    "We had all of this passion and this joy, but we needed to direct it," Simson recalls. "We needed to get the underpinning foundations of our business, otherwise it was going to be chaos and we weren't going to be able to grow the way we needed to be able to grow."

    This story illustrates why you need both a Big Vision and smaller goals along the way. Imagine your team scaling Mount Everest. Knowing your ultimate goal helps you make decisions about which base camps to stop at along your trek, pack the correct gear, get the right people on board, and do the effective preparation you need to do to reach the peak.

4. **Create a strategic blueprint:** When we lead our clients through strategic planning sessions, we use a Marketing Blueprint™—a visual planning tool that takes place of the tired old traditional marketing plan.

   We developed the Marketing Blueprint™ because we found traditional marketing and business plans too static: companies invest time and resources to create a comprehensive document that explains in lengthy narrative how the company would tackle its strategic objectives.

   That approach may have worked a decade or more ago, but with the rapid evolution of technology—for everything from social media for marketing to internal software to drive operations—organizational goals change frequently. Because things shift so quickly, these traditional documents might be obsolete the day after they're created.

   The blueprint, in contrast to a marketing or business plan, is intended to flex with a company's needs. You'll be laying out two to four major initiatives, much like you would using a more traditional approach, but you will *also* be identifying a flexible set of tactics—and these can and should change as market conditions shift and other game-changing situations arise.

   The blueprint is a visual document that invites people to write on it, update it, and revise it as needed. It can be hung on the wall, or can be used as a digital reminder.

   There is space on the blueprint for three to four initiatives/strategies with spaces for goals and tactics underneath each action item. All of these items—whether they are initiatives, goals, or tactics—should be in alignment with your mission, values, and vision:

- **Initiatives** are the overarching categories or "buckets" that exist to organize a narrower set of actionable goals.

- **Goals** are the actionable activities that, together, form each initiative. We use the acronym SMART to guide our goal-setting—in other words, goals should be:
  - Specific
  - Measurable
  - Actionable
  - Realistic
  - Time-based

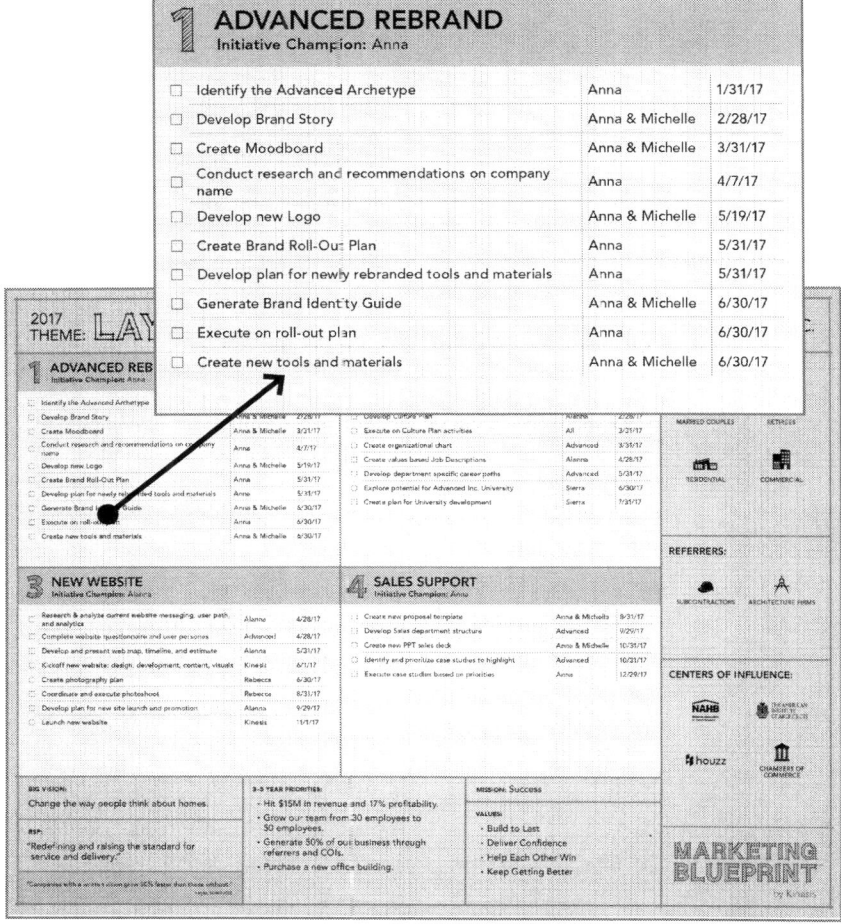

Sample initiative and goals as part of a larger Marketing Blueprint™

Initiatives

Let's start with your initiatives or strategies. Limiting the number of major initiatives to two to four is key: while it may be tempting to set more, it's simply too many for a company to handle over just six to twelve months.

Examples of initiatives could include:

- Expand our company offerings by expanding into [insert name of neighboring state].
- Develop an internal program for training hires that we bring in fresh out of high school.
- Develop a new revenue stream to sell to our existing customers.
- Find a new market segment that will purchase one of our existing offerings.
- Improve our hiring process to attract top-notch candidates from the Millennial cohort.
- Develop our Service Delivery Map.
- Create and launch our first productized service.

The following questions can help you identify your own major initiatives and then break them down into specific six- to twelve-month goals (or parts of goals):

- Where is the company right now?
- Where do we want to be in [time frame]?
- How will we get there?
- What will help us along the way?
- What moves do we need to make to succeed?
- How do we measure our progress?

Prioritizing goals

The larger the initiative, the more you should break each down into bite-sized goals—which you will then prioritize. Some of the goals under each initiative will be SMART goals and others will be what we call "outcome-based goals." In other words, some of your initiatives will be brand-new concepts and you may not yet know how to measure success other than in terms of the big-picture outcome you hope to achieve. You can create SMART goals for these once you have further fleshed out your concepts.

For instance, say you want to develop a new revenue stream to sell to existing customers. Chances are, you won't be able to highlight all the goals related to that objective quite yet—you won't yet be able to identify projected revenues or costs, for example.

An outcome-based goal might then be: "Create plan for surveying current customers about their needs" or "Analyze current marketplace to find gaps in service lines." Each of these outcome-based goals will result in a number of additional sub-goals and activities that can be made SMART as you learn more.

Below are some examples of initiatives on the blueprint. You'll see beneath the same initiative there are both SMART goals and outcome-based goals. At the top, there is the name of the initiative. Don't be too concerned about what you call it, as long as it makes sense to your team. For example, if one of your strategic objectives involves developing a new website, then you might name the initiative "website." Just keep it simple. The important thing is that your team and people have a shared language to discuss during the initiative's implementation.

5. **Delegate responsibility:** You'll notice the blueprint includes a place for a name next to each initiative. We call this person the "Initiative Lead."

This person will be responsible for moving the initiative forward and ensuring all of the goals below it are completed by their deadlines. The Initiative Lead is typically someone in a leadership position (or you may be teaching them leadership skills by given them "ownership" of the initiative).

They can either delegate the work or do it themselves if it makes sense in your organization. But at the end of the day (when the deadlines come due), the responsibility lies in this person's hands. As the sign on Harry S. Truman's desk read: "The buck stops here"—an Initiative Lead can't "pass the buck" or evade responsibility. The failure or success of an initiative is up to them.

Now look to the right of each goal: there is a space for another individual's name and a date. That person—the "Goal Lead"—is responsible for getting the goal completed by the deadline listed. Depending on the goal, they may be working solo—or they may be heading up a small team or an entire committee. It really depends on what needs to get done and the elements that the specific goal requires for completion.

The Initiative Lead will work with each Goal Lead to move the entire initiative forward. Essentially all of the Goal Leads are the Initiative Lead's direct reports, and it's up to leadership to make sure that responsibility cascades throughout your organization. (Please note: Initiative Leads and Goal Leads do not have to be a part of the strategic planning session.)

Establishing this chain of command is essential to the successful implementation of your strategic plan. A hierarchy is important because it forces leadership to communicate with employees about strategy, and it shifts the responsibility to everyone in the organization. Ideally your managers will be involved in the process and they will help present your strategy in a way that's relevant to their functional areas or departments.

Delegating responsibility when it comes to strategic initiatives brings everyone in your organization closer to the mission or core purpose of your company—and that level of engagement can be a real game-changer. That's why it's essential to always tie things back to your mission, values, and vision.

As cofounder and co-CEO of Whole Foods Market John Mackey has said, companies with a "higher purpose" inspire employees to make bolder decisions and reach their greatest potential.

"Businesses in the twenty-first century need to shift focus from profit maximization to purpose maximization," he said. By fully aligning your organization's strategies, systems, and structures around a higher purpose, he said, you will almost certainly realize business results—"making more money than you thought possible."

Case in point, Whole Foods started out as a nineteen-person grocery store in Austin, Texas, and has since grown to be the largest natural foods chain. In fact, it's one of the country's most successful retailers—with revenues doubling and profits tripling between 2007 and 2014—defying dismal grocery industry trends by offering consumers a mix of organics, delicious prepared foods, and more traditional household staples.[70] And Whole Foods was recently acquired by Amazon.com, Inc. for $13.7 billion with John Mackey still operating as CEO of the business and continuing his focus on purposeful action and living their mission.

6. **Stay focused, flexible, and within scope:** An initiative can be a huge endeavor, so when you are setting goals, never forget to focus only on activities you will be completing in the next six- to twelve-month period. Resist the temptation to extend goals farther into the future—and if you can keep them within six months, even better.

Create a new Marketing Blueprint™ at each strategic planning session, and if you haven't completed an initiative, simply add the same initiative to the new blueprint with updated goals. Once an initiative is fully completed or has become a systematic component of the business, then (and only then) you can move it off your blueprint.

Remember while you know what your overarching strategic objectives are, you don't know how market conditions, competitive pressures, or any of a number of other factors will affect your goals and activities. Breaking each initiative into small "bite-sized" tactics allow you a lot of flexibility.

As you move through goals, check them off on your blueprint. If you miss a deadline due to something that you hadn't foreseen, be sure to set a new date for the missed goal. In your next strategic planning session, you can set new six- to twelve-month goals and create new tactics that will continue moving your company toward your overarching strategic objectives, five-year goals, and Big Vision. Each initiative should remain on your blueprint until one of two things happens:

1. *The initiative is complete.* Take, for example, an initiative like the creation of a website—it can be designed and programmed within six months. However, your company may consider a second stage that includes tactics like updating your website and working on promotional endeavors. When you have carried out all the tactics and completed all the goals related to the initiative, you can replace it with a new initiative.

2. *The initiative is operationalized.* This is very important. In most cases, the initiatives that you are working on will have components that need to be woven into the fabric of your organization. So be sure to include specific goals that will make your activities

260

a long-standing and integral part of your business moving forward. This mind-set is what will evoke real, long-lasting change in your company.

One of our clients created an initiative that focused on developing a process around regularly asking for referrals from clients, employees, and business partners. We developed goals that systematized the referral request process so that it became a core part of the way various departments conducted business. Once this was implemented and a part of day-to-day operations, we moved it off the blueprint.

At each annual and semi-annual planning session after the inaugural one, you can review your blueprint and determine which initiatives have been completed or operationalized. These will move off the blueprint to make room for a new initiative. And we'll remind you—even though it may be tempting, don't have more than a total of four initiatives on your blueprint at any one time.

When it comes to initiatives that are not completed, use your strategic planning sessions to eliminate, revise, and add new goals as necessary. Make sure to appoint leads and create due dates for each new goal.

STEP THREE. Keep initiatives moving forward with a regular meeting rhythm.

Once you have completed your strategic planning session, it's essential that you set up internal meeting rhythms for the following year. Your schedule can look something like this:

- Strategic planning session (once or twice a year)
- Quarterly check-ins to see how major strategic initiatives are

progressing (this can include rolling out your mission, vision, and values, for example)

- Monthly (at least) leadership meetings to check in on departmental progress of initiatives
- Weekly meetings of small committees focused on implementing each goal

As the leaders of your organization, it's essential that you permit these gatherings to happen and provide any support and guidance your Initiative Leads need to move their initiatives forward.

Some initiatives might necessitate a monthly meeting—others, weekly. The most important thing is to establish a regular time for team members to do some work *on* the business rather than simply being mired down in their daily work *in* the business.

During your regular implementation meetings, it's vital for Initiative Leads to get very specific about the work that needs to be done:

- Make sure to break down all activities into timely, digestible, and definable segments, creating a clear road map for the people working on the goals to succeed.
- Ask team members who are working on the initiative and/or goal to report on progress. Make sure team members are not getting lost or off-track.
- Address any concerns or potential revisions to plans. Assess the goals regularly to see if there are occasions to take advantage of emerging opportunities or adjustments that need to be made due to unforeseen obstacles.
- Involve leadership as appropriate—or as needed—for guidance.

What should the structure of these implementation check-in meetings look like? At Kinesis, we have developed a process we call "Bullseye Meetings" (you can apply this same methodology to all of your company's meetings):

1. ***Always set an agenda.*** Do not go into any meeting without giving every attendee a clear idea of what you will be covering.

2. ***Always assign a meeting leader.*** Typically the person who convenes the meeting will put together the agenda and lead the meeting. Even if your meeting involves two or three people, have a clear lead.

3. ***Clearly state the purpose of your meeting.*** Clearly state the purpose of the meeting in the invitation. Then when you convene for the meeting, make sure the leader starts the session with some variation on the statement, "The purpose of this meeting is to [state desired outcome]." If the meeting goes off topic, the leader should remind the group of the meeting's purpose.

4. ***Start and end the meeting on time.*** Your meeting leader is responsible for starting and ending the meeting on time. If meetings are chronically five to ten minutes late at your company, make every effort to stop this immediately.

5. ***Build a parking lot for off-topic ideas:*** Part of the leader's job during the meeting is to make sure the participants stay on topic, following the agenda that she or he set. Sometimes great ideas come out of a meeting on a completely different topic. Other times, problems arise that need to be addressed. However, whether positive or negative, if topics that are brought up are

not within the scope of the meeting, they should be put in the "parking lot" for a separate meeting or discussion. We've found the parking lot concept helps us to stay laser-focused during our meetings. You can keep a parking lot on the side of a whiteboard, on a flipchart paper, or in your meeting notes.

6. ***Take notes and send them out.*** At every meeting, make sure there is a note-taker. This could be the leader if she or he is adept at leading while note-taking (this is a lot easier in a small group) or someone else. For larger meetings, you may consider bringing in a support person solely to take notes.

    After the meeting, make sure that the note-taker sends out the notes as soon as they are cleaned up. These notes do not have to be a transcription. They should capture the important points and be easy for group members to scan. You can include any parking lot items in the notes.

7. ***Create action items, assigned tasks, and due dates.*** Every meeting that you hold—particularly the ones around any items related to your strategic initiatives and goals—should have action items that are assigned in the meeting and captured in the notes.

    Be a company that takes action (this will separate you from the many companies who are content with "business as usual"). Next to each action item, make sure you have a person who is responsible for completing the activity and a date that they must have it done by. At your next meeting, team members should report on their progress.

8. ***Measure, report, and update.*** In every meeting that is focused on implementation, include a small amount of time to update the group on progress. Give each Goal Lead one to two minutes

to report on the status of the goal they are responsible for completing.

At Kinesis, we structure all of our meetings using this method. This has made an enormous difference when it comes to both internal productivity and forward momentum. Here is a very simple example: One year, one of our Marketing Blueprint™ initiatives was "marketing and sales." Within this initiative was a goal that revolved around producing content for our blog.

As the Initiative Lead, our colleague Sally held a meeting with two team members working on this particular goal. Following the Bullseye Method, she set the agenda and let people know that the purpose of the meeting was to determine a schedule for the blog along with specific content for it. During the meeting, Sally gave an overview of the goal and its progress. Shortly after the meeting, she sent out the following notes via email:

Per our discussion, we decided on two Kinesis blog posts per month— along with one external publication. This list addresses the former, not the latter. Please let us know how we can help support!

FEBRUARY EDITORIAL CALENDAR

Post # 1: Why Responsive Design is Important
Target Publish Date: February 10, 2016
Buyer Cycle Stage: Awareness
Angle: Mobile browsing has officially surpassed desktop—and considering Google's "Mobilegeddon" in April of last year, any company with a nonresponsive site is at a distinct disadvantage. The post will give a brief education on responsive web design, position it within current marketing context, and give an overview of its advantages. Weave in Kinesis examples as appropriate (potentially actual metrics: changes in web traffic pre-/post-?).

Milestones:

- **Wednesday 2/3:** Jenn submits post first draft to Sally
- **Thursday 2/4:** Sally reviews & revises post
- **Friday 2/5:** Design team will select appropriate visuals for post
- **Friday 2/5:** Sally will build campaign in MailChimp
- **Monday 2/8:** Newsletter in Shawn's hands for review
- **Wednesday 2/10:** Publish & send!

As Initiative Lead, Sally was very clear on the implementation plan, deadlines, and responsibilities. She shared a list of deadlines with the individuals who were helping her, as well as with Shawn as CEO. Similarly, everyone in the organization knew what was happening with the initiative because at our larger blueprint progress meeting, she was able to provide very specific updates on the initiative progress.

STEP FOUR. Measure Progress.

Strategy is not about perfection. Rather it's about forward momentum toward your strategic objectives. That said, creating good solid measurements will help your leaders understand where their teams are in their process and how well they are doing. Ensure the metrics you set are quantifiable—they should be relevant to your goal, capable of being tracked, and owned by the Goal Lead, and ultimately the Initiative Lead. They should include a temporal component.

Here are some examples of quantifiable metrics to give you an idea of what to include:

- If your strategy and goals are financial, your team could put measurements in place such as net sales, gross profit margins, number of sales, and so on.

- If they are customer-centric, you might put into place measures such as number of customer complaints, appointment cancellations, dollars per account, number of new customers, customer churn, and so on.

- And if your strategy is employee-based, some possible measurements could include employee retention, average sales per employee, employee turnover, number of quality resumes received a week, etc.

The metrics you collect are widely varied, so the above are only illustrations and not recommendations. Don't agonize over the best metrics—start with the obvious, easy ones. And then refine and improve them over time. If you don't know what measurements are best, you could have "develop metrics" as an outcome-based goal on your blueprint.

The Strategic Planning Process: A Quick Review

Congratulations! You now have a strategic planning process and meeting rhythm structure to help you put the Marketing From the Inside Out® concepts into place in your organization. You can also use the process to move forward *anything* you would like to accomplish to help your company grow and thrive.

Here's a quick refresher course on implementing new initiatives at your organization:

1. ***Prepare for your Strategic Planning Session.*** Set a date, determine the meeting participants, and pick a meeting location. Answer the questions in this chapter and gather the necessary documents.

Ensure your team members are ready to report on progress when it comes to the initiatives and goals you discussed in your last strategic planning session. (If this is your first planning session, make sure you've reviewed the concepts in this book so you can create new initiatives around Marketing From the Inside Out® concepts.)

Put together a meeting agenda and determine what you want to accomplish during the meeting. Make sure participants are familiar with the Bullseye Meeting process to ensure you will have an effective meeting.

2. ***Set aside a day or two.*** Make sure your leadership team has the time to work on your business without being interrupted by clients or other employees. Ask people to keep their technology off and only check phones/tablets/computers during breaks.

3. ***Make sure you have your One-Word Mission™, Living, Breathing Values™, Big Vision, and three- to five-year goals in place.*** You should always bring in documents that remind your whole team of your larger strategic vision so that everyone sets initiative and goals that are in alignment with your long-term objectives.

4. ***Create three to four initiatives and related goals.*** Restrain yourself and keep your focus on only a few initiatives. You want to come back in six months with successes. If you try to achieve too many things, your team and resources will be diluted. This often results in failed implementation. (You can use the parking lot during your strategic planning meetings to put ideas that you can't get to in the next six months.)

5. ***Assign Initiative Leads and Goal Leads.*** For each initiative, make sure there is a Lead who is accountable for the initiative. At the end of the day, they are the one who "owns" it.

    Assign a Goal Lead to each goal—often this person will be fully involved in working on the goal. They are the *doer.*

6. ***Carve out company time for implementation.*** To succeed at the execution of your goals and initiatives, you must give your people the time to work on them. While this will take away from billable hours, allotting time for strategic initiatives can have a huge ROI.

7. ***Establish meeting rhythms.*** Set regular meeting rhythms with action items, assignments, and due dates. Make sure your people are having weekly or monthly meeting to "move the ball down the field." Meeting consistency is key for communication, accountability, and dynamism.

8. ***Be flexible and adapt.*** Your goals should flex in response to market opportunities or threats. This ability to nimbly adapt within your company is what will make your strategic objectives successful. Use our blueprint tool so you can update, revise, and move around your goals under each initiative—it's a working, evolving document that should adapt to your changing organization and marketplace

9. ***Measure results.*** If you aren't in the habit of measuring things, start today. Even if you don't have progress to measure, starting today will give you baseline data. For all goals moving forward, have key performance indicators and metrics that will help your company know the impact of your efforts. Review metrics and improve your activities based on what you learn.

EPILOGUE

YOU NOW HAVE MANY TOOLS THAT MOST OTHER SMALL and mid-sized businesses do not. The Marketing From the Inside Out® process has worked for Kinesis and for many of our clients—and we hope it will work for you.

You have read through this entire book and you now have a choice to make. We encourage you to choose to be remarkable. We hope you want to build a company where everyone—including you—is thrilled to come to work each day, the kind of company people rave about.

While it may feel risky to be remarkable, being mediocre is a far greater risk. Remarkability will give you the competitive advantage now—and well into the future.

It's up to each one of us to make this world a better place—one we want to live in and one we want to work in. It is our hope that you now have the tools to make that a reality in your company. We wish you the absolute best in your journey.

NOTES

PREFACE

1. U.S. Small Business Administration, Office of Advocacy, Frequently Asked Questions, Question #6 at https://www.sba.gov/sites/default/files/advocacy/SB-FAQ-2016_WEB.pdf
2. A Web 2.0 website may allow users to interact and collaborate with each other in a social media dialogue as creators of user-generated content in a virtual community, in contrast to the first generation of Web 1.0-era websites where people were limited to the passive viewing of content.

INTRODUCTION

3. http://www.colorado.edu/studentgroups/libertarians/issues/friedman-soc-resp-business.html
4. http://www.sfu.ca/~wainwrig/Econ400/jensen-meckling.pdf
5. http://www.colorado.edu/studentgroups/libertarians/issues/friedman-soc-resp-business.html
6. http://www.forbes.com/sites/stevedenning/2014/10/14/the-unanticipated-risks-of-maximizing-shareholder-value/#6296bb675214
7. http://www.forbes.com/sites/stevedenning/2014/10/14/the-unanticipated-risks-of-maximizing-shareholder-value/#74d3c2735214
8. https://www.ft.com/content/294ff1f2-0f27-11de-ba10-0000779fd2ac

PRINCIPLE #1

9. http://engageforsuccess.org/case-study-alcoa-power-and-propulsion-best-employee-engagement-initiative-winners
10. http://www.npr.org/2016/10/04/496508361/former-wells-fargo-employees-describe-toxic-sales-culture-even-at-hq
11. https://www.theglobeandmail.com/report-on-business/the-testing-of-michael-mccain/article598005/
12. https://www.ft.com/content/8c8d3668-adb5-11e2-82b8-00144feabdc0

PRINCIPLE #2

13. Margaret Heffernan, "The Moral of the Story," *Fast Company,* last modified: March 1, 2005, http://www.fastcompany.com/55275/morale-story

14. https://www2.deloitte.com/us/en/pages/about-deloitte/articles/culture-of-purpose.html

15. "State of the Global Workplace Employee Engagement Insights for Business Leaders Worldwide," Gallup, Inc., 2013.

16. http://www.fedweek.com/federal-managers-daily-report/nasa-retains-top-ranking-place-work/

17. https://www.newyorker.com/magazine/2012/04/09/gusher

18. https://www.nytimes.com/2015/07/02/business/exxon-lumbers-along-to-catch-up-with-gay-rights.html

PRINCIPLE #3

19. https://hbr.org/2002/07/make-your-values-mean-something.html

20. http://www.gallup.com/businessjournal/195491/few-employees-believe-company-values.aspx

21. http://www.gallup.com/businessjournal/195506/few-workers-apply-company-values-jobs.aspx

22. http://tompeters.com/2007/02/whats-culture-got-to-do-with-it/

PRINCIPLE #4

23. http://www.inc.com/magazine/20110201/creating-a-company-vision.html

24. www.smh.com.au/small-business/entrepreneur/redballoons-vision-was-no-flight-of-fancy-20120401-1w6gs.html

25. http://history.nasa.gov/Apollomon/Apollo.html

PRINCIPLE #5

26. porterconsultingnet/index.php/category/channel-sales/page/3/

27. https://www.youtube.com/watch?v=gGaeYwsa6h4 Anjali Lai, Forrester Customer Experience Index talk, 2015.

28. Cialdini, Robert B., "Harnessing the Science of Persuasion," *Harvard Business Review* 79 (9): 72–79, October 2001.

29. http://www.marketingcharts.com/traditional/only-1-in-2-companies-say-sales-marketing-have-a-formal-definition-of-a-qualified-lead-39775/

PRINCIPLE #6

30. http://blog.alphaarchitect.com/2015/09/15/buffett-economic-moats/#gs.9UVTq7Y

31. www.manpowergroup.com/talent-shortage-explorer/ #.WkwOgiOZOCS

32. http://variety.com/2013/biz/news/epic-fail-how-blockbuster-could-have-owned-netflix-1200823443/

33. James C. Wetherbe, "The World on Time: The 11 Management Principles That Made FedEx an Overnight Sensation."

34. David S. Kidder, *The Startup Playbook: Secrets of the Fastest-Growing Startups from Their Founding Entrepreneurs* (San Francisco: Chronicle Books, 2013).

35. http://www.forbes.com/sites/micahsolomon/2015/02/18/the-rackspace-method-fanatical-customer-service-and-customer-support-in-the-b2b-cloud/

PRINCIPLE #7

36. https://www.cmocouncil.org/thought-leadership/reports/btob-content-impacts-customer-thinking--buying-decisions

37. http://www2.pardot.com/l/1/2013-09-26/2tjcfk

PRINCIPLE #8

38. Forbes Insights and Sitecore, "Customers for Life: Technology Strategies for Attracting and Keeping Customers," 2014.

39. Farris, Paul W. et al., *Marketing Metrics: The Definitive Guide to Measuring Marketing Performance* (Indianapolis, IN: Pearson FT Press, 2010).

40. Reichheld, F., and W. E. Sasser Jr. "Zero Defections: Quality Comes to Services," *Harvard Business Review* 68, no. 5 (September–October 1990).

41. *2011 Customer Experience Impact Report*, conducted by Harris Interactive, commissioned by RightNow.

42. http://www.huffingtonpost.com/young-entrepreneur-council/3-advantages-of-monthly-r_b_8831002.html

43. https://www.chargify.com/blog/subscription-business-trend-predictions-for-2016/

44. https://archive.ama.org/Archive/AboutAMA/Pages/AMA%20Publications/AMA%20Journals/Journal%20of%20Marketing/TOCs/SUM_2009.5/Effects_of_Word-of-Mouth.aspx

45. https://hbr.org/2011/06/why-customer-referrals-can-drive-stunning-profits

PRINCIPLE #9

46. http://www.1to1media.com/employee-engagement-strategies/united-airlines-proves-improving-customer-experience-requires

47. https://www.bloomberg.com/features/2016-united-airlines-struggles/

48. http://www.chicagotribune.com/business/ct-airlines-twitter-0602-biz-20150601-story.html

49. http://heidicohen.com/social-media-needs-customer-service/

50. http://www.davecarrollmusic.com/songwriting/united-breaks-guitars/

51. https://www.accenture.com/t20150624T211502__w__/us-en/_acnmedia/Accenture/Conversion-Assets/DotCom/Documents/Global/PDF/Industries_15/Accenture-B2B-Procurement-Study.pdf

52. http://about.americanexpress.com/news/docs/2014x/2014-Global-Customer-Service-Barometer-US.pdf
53. Fred Reichheld, "Prescription for Cutting Costs," Bain and Company, Inc.
54. http://www.ccsenet.org/journal/index.php/ijbm/article/viewFile/6745/6332/
55. https://www.strativity.com/wp-content/uploads/2014/08/Engaged-Employees-Deliver-Higher-Customer-Satisfaction.pdf?vsmaid=140&vcid=3036
56. http://www.bain.com/publications/articles/the-chemistry-of-enthusiasm.aspx
57. http://hbr.org/2012/05/to-keep-your-customers-keep-it-simple/ar/1
58. McKinsey and Company, "The 'moment of truth' in customer service," *McKinsey Quarterly*, February 2006.
59. Gallup, "State of the American Consumer: Insights for Business Leaders," 2014.
60. http://www.tandfonline.com/doi/abs/10.1080/01449290500330448
61. http://credibility.stanford.edu/guidelines/index.html
62. http://www.clarityqst.com/three-hallmarks-of-effective-web-design-to-convert-b2b-customers/
63. Google/Millward Brown Digital, B2B Path to Purchase Study, 2014.
64. http://www.sciencedirect.com/science/article/pii/S095354381100035X
65. http://www.jstor.org/stable/2393794?seq=1#page_scan_tab_contents
66. http://www.upi.com/Health_News/2010/12/11/Study-First-impression-has-lasting-impact/UPI-70801292049847/
67. https://hbr.org/2012/07/the-end-of-solution-sales

PRINCIPLE #10

68. http://www.mckinsey.com/insights/strategy/how_to_improve_strategic_planning
69. http://www.mckinsey.com/insights/strategy/tired_of_strategic_planning
70. http://fortune.com/2014/04/10/whole-foods-takes-over-america/

35772857R00161

Made in the USA
Middletown, DE
08 February 2019